"In the 80s, I went on my own journey to be ¦ this book, *Healing Rain*, had been written ¦ has written the keys to physical and mental to dig out of many sources, not to mentioi. prayer. If you are fighting against anxiety and depression, this book has keys to finding wholeness and peace. If you are desperately needing physical healing, there are deep truths that will help lead to the miracle you need."

Cindy Jacobs, co-founder, Generals International

"Sue Detweiler's new book, *Healing Rain: Immersing Yourself in Christ's Love to Find Wholeness of Mind, Body, and Heart*, is a book of encouragement that forms a basis of hope on the experience and understanding of God's love, and the understanding of who He is in us and who we are in Him. Sue helps us to understand the Father's love for us, Jesus Christ's redemptive work on our behalf, and the Holy Spirit's empowerment for service, healing, and miracles."

Dr. Randy Clark, overseer of the apostolic network of Global Awakening, president of Global Awakening Theological Seminary

"*Healing Rain* is a solid, anointed teaching focusing on the complete healing of body, soul, and spirit. Such powerful scriptural revelation with solid applicable wisdom. Read this message, apply its truths, and walk the abundant life of God's healing power and love. Thank you, Sue, for this timely, empowering, life-transforming word."

Rebecca Greenwood, president and co-founder of Christian Harvest International

"The Lord is raising up a company of lover warriors in this day of darkness, conflict, glory, and awakening. The earth may be preparing for war, but heaven is preparing for a wedding. Hence, it is our hearts the Lord is most interested in. He calls loving Him and others the Great Commandment and implores us to guard our heart with all diligence for out of it springs the issue of life (Proverbs 4:23). Sue Detweiler's *Healing Rain* skillfully delves into healing for the whole of who we are—spirit, soul, and body—enabling us to arise healed and victorious with our eyes on the prize of Jesus Christ."

Patricia Bootsma, national outreach director, Catch the Fire USA; global prayer director, JH Israel

"Pressing with hunger and passion into God's wisdom and command in Proverbs to guard your heart with all vigilance, *Healing Rain* will take you back to the center of it all—to where the 'wellsprings of life' flow from and where the battle is won or lost (see Proverbs 4:23). I believe you will be strengthened by the specific action steps and insightful prayer primers Sue offers, aligning you for loyal and wholehearted abandonment to Jesus."

Dana Candler, IHOPKC leadership, author
of First Love and Deep unto Deep

"The Body of Christ is desperate for ministers of healing! Thank God for Sue Detweiler and her book Healing Rain. I know it can lead many hurting people into wholeness and help them maintain a lifetime of divine health. Blessings!"

Joan Hunter, evangelist, host of Miracles Happen!

"Jesus heals. He heals bodies, hearts, and lives. Sue Detweiler's book Healing Rain is a testimony of Jesus, whose salvation includes healing, deliverance, and wholeness. Sue masterfully weaves together biblical truth with personal testimony to reveal that Jesus, our savior, healer, and deliverer, is the same yesterday, today, and forever."

Kim Maas, CEO and founder of Kim Maas Ministries, Inc.

"Sue Detweiler carries the fire of God's presence, which transforms lives. As a part of the UPPERROOM community, Sue has immersed herself in Christ's love and found wholeness of mind, body, and heart. Healing Rain is an equipping tool for individual and corporate revival. If you are on a healing journey, Healing Rain will guide you on a pathway to be soaked in His presence, healed by His Word, and strengthened by His covenant."

Michael Miller, founder and senior pastor of UPPERROOM

"Do you believe in miracles but are experiencing a healing crisis as you wait on God? So did many of the healing greats named in this book, so did I, and so did Sue! Get ready to heal your head, address burnout, stop agreeing with sickness, and activate your faith!"

Laura Harris Smith, N.D., naturopathic doctor,
author, host of theTHREE

"If you're in a fight of faith to overcome physical infirmity, this may be just the book for you. Sue's message carries authority because she speaks from the context of her own fiery trials and how the Lord has supernaturally healed her. Sue's irrepressible personality comes through delightfully in every chapter. Your faith will be strengthened, and you'll gain renewed understanding for the pathway before you. Receive grace to both run and overcome!"

Bob Sorge, author of The Fire of Delayed Answers

Healing RAIN

IMMERSING YOURSELF IN CHRIST'S LOVE
TO FIND WHOLENESS OF
MIND, BODY, AND HEART

SUE DETWEILER

Chosen
a division of Baker Publishing Group
Minneapolis, Minnesota

To Apostle Guillermo Maldonado,
father to the nations,
who is bringing supernatural power
to this generation.

To Randy Clark,
carrier of revival fire to the nations,
who laid hands on me and said,
"Electrocute her, Jesus."

To Michael and Lorisa Miller,
who have stewarded the transformative
presence of Jesus and called a generation
to die so that they may fully live.

To Leif Hetland,
who transparently carries the baptism of love,
spurring me on to receive from Papa God.

To John and Paula Sandford,
who taught me to seek inner healing
and to pray more than I say.

To John Wimber,
who taught me how to pray
for the sick and cast out demons.

To Maria Woodworth Etter,
Aimee Semple McPherson,
and Kathryn Kuhlman,
who taught me to believe
in the God of miracles.

Healing Rain

VERSE 1

Soak me with Your presence
Cleanse me with Your love
Fill me with Your power
Healing Rain

VERSE 2

Refresh me with Your Spirit
Restore me with Your Word
Immerse me in Your truth
Healing Rain, fall on me

CHORUS

Healing Rain, fall on me
Flood my heart, fill my need
Healing Rain, fall on me
Healing Rain, set me free

VERSE 3

Receive my cry to heaven
As I fall down to my knees
Purify Your people
Healing Rain, fall on me

BRIDGE

The sea will part; the blind will see
The storm will still; the lame will leap
The giants fall; the dead will rise
Kingdom reign released

Contents

Foreword 11

Acknowledgments 13

Introduction: *Awakened to the Supernatural Realm* 15

1. Turning Point 23
   The Journey to Embrace Jesus as Healer

2. R.E.S.T. 36
   Revive Expectancy, Surrender, and Trust

3. Heal Your Head 54
   Transform the Way You Think

4. Covenant 62
   The Promise of Health and Wholeness

5. Gateway 74
   Experiencing the Power of Communion

6. A Troubled Heart 85
   The Trap of Disappointment, Sorrow, and Loss

7. Surrender 100
   Positioning Your Heart to Be Healed

8. Loosed   107
   Set Free from a Spirit of Infirmity

9. Freed   121
   Deliverance out of Darkness, into Light

10. Faith   131
    Moving Mountains through Prayer

11. Stand   145
    Persevering for Divine Healing

12. Wholeness   156
    Immersed in the Father's Love

13. Prevail   168
    Embracing Time with Jesus

14. Anointing to Heal   174
    Soaking in His Presence

Afterword: *A Call for Spiritual Fathers
   and Mothers*   181
Begin a *Healing Rain* Study
   Group   189
Group Discussion Guide   193
Notes   199

Foreword

I am pleased to write this foreword for Sue Detweiler, a woman of God who demonstrates her great love for the Lord by maintaining a deep, intimate relationship with our heavenly Father, His Son Jesus Christ, and the Holy Spirit. As she states, her book *Healing Rain* aims to transform stony hearts into fertile soil capable of bearing good fruit for the Kingdom of heaven. It is excellent to know that the author followed the promptings of the Holy Spirit and poured all the divine revelation she received and her abundant personal experience into this book. The objective is to guide others toward healing their spirit, soul, and body, having a truly intimate relationship with our heavenly Father.

In this end time, before the coming of Christ, the Church owes the world an experience with God. The Church has offered doctrines, dogmas, rites, and theology for a long time, but little experience with His presence. We need more books that talk about our experiences with God. However, this can only be obtained by seeking God in prayer or spending time with Him, not only amid life's trials and afflictions but at all times and under all circumstances.

Sue does a wonderful job in this regard. She has gathered spiritual wisdom through her trials, has been flexible, and has allowed herself to be formed without departing from the faith. All of this has given her a broad experience with God that can inspire others to seek the same.

Sue writes about topics that are fundamental to me and that are at the core of my most recent books, such as the importance of cultivating an intimate relationship with God, faith, covenant with God, changing mindsets, deliverance from diseases and the role of demons in them, and the power that Jesus released on the cross so that we can forgive and be forgiven, be set free, and receive inner healing and deliverance.

Sue has not forgotten that every believer can be empowered and used by God to perform miracles. We must be prepared to go and impart that power to others who need it. But most of all, Sue challenges Christ's Church to be a true body that puts into practice spiritual exercises that have been left on the back burner, such as prayer, fasting, and faith, and allows us to walk in God's supernatural power.

Healing Rain is a powerful book that I highly recommend. Sue has written a practical guide to developing an intimate relationship with God. It includes several concepts and principles I have always believed in, written about, and walked out throughout my life. God is not a theory or a religion; He is our heavenly Father, and He longs to have a living experience with us—His children and His creation—until we come to have an eternal, continuous, and growing relationship like the one Jesus had with Him. As I express in my book *Cultivating an Intimate Relationship with God*, we need to know Him to have that relationship with our heavenly Father. We need to relate to Him because our relationship with God is based on love, obedience, fear of God, trust, communication, and commitment.

Sue Detweiler's *Healing Rain* is set to become a catalyst for end-time revival. Jesus is coming back soon, and He is coming for a church without spot or wrinkle, with an ongoing relationship with Him and fully committed to advancing His Kingdom. Be assured that you are ready to receive Him!

Apostle Guillermo Maldonado
King Jesus International Ministry, Miami, Florida

Acknowledgments

Writing a book on healing implies that I've been through suffering, pain, and loss. I want to thank everyone who has been on my "healing team," including Elizabeth Reed and Dani Williamson. Thank you for your compassionate hearts, wise counsel, and medical expertise. Thank you also to my "prayer shield," those of you who pray for me when I'm in the nations and prayed with me to complete this book on healing. Thank you to spiritual children worldwide who asked for this book to be written. Thank you, Kellie Copeland, Susie Larson, and Tara Seidman; your friendship has enriched me.

Who knew I would travel the world as a Mimi with eight grandchildren at home? Thanks to AW, EK, CJ, WB, EF, CR, JD, and miracle baby JA for multiplying my joy. I loved sending pictures and videos of lions, giraffes, zebras, crocodiles, hippopotamuses, and other kinds of animals your way when I was in Africa. To my children, Rachel and Dustin, Angela and Bryan, Hannah and Dustin, Sarah Faith, Dre (in heaven), and Zeke, I pray that you would each walk in the supernatural power of God in your daily lives. Gigi, thanks for being a woman of prayer. I can hear you praying in tongues at 4:00 a.m. in your Eagle's Nest, and it brings joy, peace, and comfort to my heart.

A writer needs a team of people who believe in you and the writing project; thank you to the Chosen team, including Kim Bangs and Trish Konieczny, for partnering with the supernatural power of God to see *Healing Rain* completed. Thank you, Pastor Dale Evrist and Marianne Adams, for cowriting the song "Healing Rain," which has carried the heart of healing to the nations. Thank you, Pastor Dale, for imparting the love of God's Word and the fear of the Lord.

Thank you to every *Healing Rain* guest who first shared your story on the podcast, which people now listen to in 135 nations. Thank you for sharing your transformational story in this book: Dana Candler, Lauri Carnahan, Donna Graber, Pastor Alejandro Morales, Heidi Mortenson, Gretchen Rodriguez, Jared Scott, Sean Smith Sr., Bob Sorge, Sherry Stahl, Kimberly Stokes, Leslie Tracey, Evelyn Williams, and Pastor Silas and Pastora Carmen Zdrojewski. Thank you also to Joan Hunter, who shared her story that brings insight on going to the root of trauma, healing hearts and bodies.

As I began to travel internationally regularly, I cried out to God for spiritual fathers. Thank you, Randy Clark, Global Awakening Team, and students at Global Awakening Theological Seminary (GATS) for imparting the fire of revival. Thank you, Apostle Guillermo Maldonado and Supernatural Global Network, for imparting signs, wonders, and miracles to the nations. Thank you, Leif Hetland and Global Mission Awareness Team, for leading me to rest in the arms of Papa God. Thank you also, Michael Miller and the UPPERROOM community, for carrying His transformative presence that brought healing to my heart and body.

Thank you most of all to my husband, Wayne Detweiler, the love of my life, healing shepherd, and forever friend. Before you proposed marriage, you looked in my eyes and said, "I know you have a call of God on your life; I will do everything I can to release you to the Body of Christ and the nations." You prophesied that I would write many books before I believed it in my heart. Your reward is eternal.

Introduction

Awakened to the Supernatural Realm

Have you awakened from the dead of night into a supernatural fight between life and death? I remember dropping to my knees when I could not escape from my house set ablaze by an arsonist's hand. I prayed the prayer that everyone prays when they believe they will die: *Help!*

I would have died in that fire, unable to save my five-week-old baby, Rachel, if it hadn't been for the obedience of my mother to fast, pray, and meditate on Isaiah 43 weeks before the fire occurred. God answered her miraculous prayer: *"When you walk through the fire, you will not be burned; the flames will not set you ablaze"* (Isaiah 43:2 NIV).

An arsonist had set the home next to us on fire, and our home was also set ablaze while Rachel and I slept. We had been robbed a few weeks earlier, and it became clear that someone had been watching our home. We were young pastors, planting our first church in Nashville, Tennessee.

The night of the fire, angels guided my husband home just in time. Angels also showed the fireman how to fight through the demonic assault to find me and say, "Come toward the light."[1]

It was a miracle that our baby didn't suffer long-term physical damage from the lack of oxygen to her brain and the vital organs of her five-week-old body. Rachel Joy survived the fire and thrived.

These miracles were just the beginning of the healing and deliverance that Jesus brought into our lives through this traumatic and life-changing event.

Going Deeper with God

Has trauma or sickness caused you to cry out to God? The trauma of the fire and the aftermath of rebuilding and recovering made my husband, Wayne, and me realize that our current relationship with Jesus wasn't deep enough to deliver us from our present struggle. Targeted by witchcraft, we were being watched. When my husband left, the phone would ring, and I would hear heavy breathing on the other end of the line. Two months after the fire, I got a phone call at 3:00 a.m. and heard a blood-curdling laugh from a woman who sounded like a witch. It put terror in my heart.

I had been traumatized by the fire. I would wake up when Rachel cried and immediately start sprinting to her crib, feeling the panic of not being able to get her. The smell of smoke would trigger me to have flashbacks where I experienced the helplessness of being trapped.

Even though we loved Jesus and were pastoring a church, our desperation to find healing from trauma drove us to seek help. Miracles are often a beginning for you and me to dive deeper into God's presence. When you are helpless and know that the only answer for you and your marriage is Jesus, that's the beginning of a transformation.

We finally found help at an Inner Healing and Deliverance conference for pastors and leaders. We thought we were going to the conference to deal with the trauma caused by the fire, but God took us deeper.

In the session Wayne attended, he was ministered to for healing the wounds of having sexual intercourse as a teenager. His breakthrough led to a transformation of our love life and the revitalization of our marriage relationship.

When I went to the conference, I knew that I needed to forgive the arsonist who had set our house on fire. But Father God took me deeper. He led me to repent of some of the liberal theology that had penetrated my heart through seminary training. Revival broke out in my heart as I repented of my unbelief. I also forgave the person who had sexually abused me as a child. Jesus freed me that day of demons of religion and rejection. Revived with freedom and joy, I have never been the same.

Hearts Ablaze for Jesus

With our newfound freedom, Wayne and I were both on fire for Jesus. Revival had come to our hearts and home, and now we couldn't help but share this with others. From that point forward, we ministered healing and deliverance regularly. We also began to walk in the gifts of the Holy Spirit every day, seeing the miraculous regularly.

I began to pray and prophesy over strangers whom I didn't know or had just met. The Holy Spirit would instruct me to stop at a gas station to give someone a word of knowledge and pray for healing.

Most women who had difficulty conceiving got pregnant after I prayed for them. Ankles and backs were healed, deaf ears opened. I will tell some of these stories in the chapters ahead.

These healings happened at church, but they also happened on the streets. Miraculous living can be your everyday Christian life, just as it became mine.

In *Healing Rain*, we will explore three categories of healing:

1. *Inner healing* of your heart, which includes your mind, will, and emotions. At times, I will describe this as "heart healing."
2. *Spiritual healing*, which begins with the miracle of rebirth or salvation. Spiritual healing also includes deliverance from demons.
3. *Physical healing* of your body.

Cultivate Your Heart for Revival

The purpose of *Healing Rain* is to cultivate a miraculous culture in the soil of your heart. This book will help you grow a healthy heart culture by breaking up the hard ground and removing the weeds. It will soak the soil of your heart to prepare you to be a carrier of revival. Here are some other things this book will do:

Healing Rain invites you into a miraculous adventure with Jesus every day. Cultivation is a combination of removing weeds from the garden of your heart and loosening the soil to improve the retention and penetration of God's Word, His will, and His ways.

Healing Rain invites you to break agreement with the enemy in your thoughts and actions. Through our mindsets and the postures of our hearts, we can receive the seed of God's Word, which will bear life-giving fruit.

Healing Rain will help you identify the lies and false narratives planted by the enemy.

Healing Rain will initiate a downpour of God's refreshing presence, love, and power. You will be led on a journey of turning away from self-reliance and seeking what only comes from Jesus. "So now you need to rethink

everything and turn to God so your sins will be forgiven
and a new day can dawn, days of refreshing times flowing
from the Lord. Then God may send Jesus the Anointed,
whom God has chosen for you" (Acts 3:19–20 VOICE).

Healing Rain will lead you to turn away from religious rules
or a rebellious heart and run into the waiting arms of the
Father. You will find new freedom in your thoughts and
emotions. You will find healing not only in your body, but
also in your soul and spirit.

Healing Rain will include for you some powerfully encouraging testimonies from people who have experienced divine
health and healing in miraculous ways. Many of these
stories (edited for inclusion here) come from interviews I
did on my *Healing Rain* podcast.

Healing Rain will unlock the supernatural through what I
call "7 keys to divine health." You will be able to access
these keys that will open the door to the supernatural in
your life:

—*The key of freedom* gives you the authority to make good
choices with your will.

—*The key of connection* opens the door to right standing
with God.

—*The key of health* gives you victory over your physical
infirmities.

—*The key of prosperity* brings you victory over mental torment and physical poverty.

—*The key of influence* gives you authority over every area
of your life, home, and work.

—*The key of purity* gives you victory over your internal
pain and suffering.

—*The key of rest* signifies that Jesus won back our eternal
joy and healed us of our broken hearts.

Jesus Wants to Revive You

Healing Rain is a book about intimacy with the Father, the Son, and the Holy Spirit. Jesus wants to revive you—revive your heart, your home, and your community. Use this book as a spiritual surfboard. It is simply a small platform upon which you can paddle out and position yourself to ride the wave of His revival that is beginning to move across the nations. As you catch the wave of the Holy Spirit, allow joy and refreshment to drench your life with His presence.

Healing Rain will help you develop the character needed to sustain a move of God in your heart, your home, and your community. Cultivating inner purity in your heart will open the way for extreme power in your life. If you would like to go deeper and immerse yourself even more fully in God's healing rain, make sure to take time along the way to do the "Healing Moments for Your Heart and Health" and "Diving Deeper in God's Word" exercises you will find interspersed throughout the chapters ahead. They will help you reflect on and apply the healing concepts we are talking about. You could also begin a *Healing Rain* study group, where you and others can take that deeper dive together and learn more about the concepts in this book. There's more information for you about forming such a group in the section at the back called "Begin a *Healing Rain* Study Group" (which follows the Afterword).

To go even deeper, you can add video teachings to your own study, and especially to your group experience. I have made an eight-session *Healing Rain* video series available for this on my website, suedetweiler.com.² Each of the eight videos provides deeper biblical foundations, but also models how to walk in the gifts of the Holy Spirit practically. Each video carries an impartation of grace and empowerment. In this series, you will find practical examples of how to hear the voice of God, how to understand visions from God, how to prophesy, and how to heal the sick.

Experience the Miraculous Every Day

As we pursue Jesus every day, we will experience the more extraordinary miracles that He has promised. Prepare to experience the miraculous every day! As you learn how to sense and obey the Holy Spirit's promptings, the people you pray for will be transformed by the Father's love and the power of Jesus Christ. As you embrace your entire inheritance, Jesus will activate the gifts of the Holy Spirit in your life. You will learn how to take risks to minister healing in public settings, even with strangers. Your life can become a catalyst for revival in your home and community.

As we prepare for this journey of faith, be encouraged by Paul's words: "Follow the way of love and eagerly desire gifts of the Spirit, especially prophecy" (1 Corinthians 14:1 NIV). Take a moment and pray this prayer out loud:

Jesus Christ,
the Anointed One,
Bridegroom,
As I begin this journey of making You my first love
draw me closer to You as Your beautiful Bride.
I want to see You transfigured with resurrection glory
as I fellowship with You in the midst of suffering.
Purify the culture of my life.
Make the soil of my heart ready to receive Your Word
as I become a life-laid-down lover of Yours.

Daddy,
Papa God,
Father in heaven,
I surrender my preconceived ideas, fears, and anything else
that hinders me from running into the welcome of Your arms.
Shine Your light on rebellion or religion in my heart.
Thank You that there is no striving or
performance in this pursuit.

As I seek Your Kingdom and righteousness first,
all these things will be added to me (Mathew 6:33).
Thank You that I don't need to worry or fret;
I crawl into Your lap and lean my head on Your heart!

Holy Spirit,
Spirit of grace,
Advocate and Comforter,
I desperately need to be soaked in Your presence.
I don't even know all the places in my heart
that need the touch of the finger of God.
I invite You to convict me of sin,
but also to free me from condemnation.
Reveal the areas where I'm
functioning in fear rather than love.

Yahweh Rapha,
my Beloved Healer,
I lay down my burdens
during this kairos moment of encounter with You.
I bring the areas in my body that need physical healing,
and the places in my mind that need renewal,
and my broken heart that needs mending,
and relationships that need repairing.
Touch me with Your miraculous presence.
I open every area of my life to You.
In Jesus' name I pray, Amen.

one

Turning Point

The Journey to Embrace Jesus as Healer

As we cultivate a miraculous culture in the soil of our hearts, breaking up the rocky ground and pulling up the weeds is essential. In our questioning, we begin to accuse God in our hearts of *not* being a healer, or at least of not being *our* healer. The accusation comes with thoughts like these:

If God is my healer, why am I sick?
I've prayed for healing; why has God not answered my prayer?

We receive the Word of God in seed form through our mindsets and the postures of our hearts. It isn't easy to honestly believe something in a world that contradicts our personal experience.

Most of us believe that Jesus is a healer. Our main struggle is not whether Jesus heals, but is how we access His healing in our lives. When we face a physical challenge, sickness can become magnified as we deal with its burden daily. Chronic disease can become a jail cell that holds us back from the fullness of God's promises in our lives.

A Vision of Breakthrough

Taking a run on my favorite path that led to the YMCA was a daily routine. I would run a mile and a half to the YMCA, work out in a class or lift weights, and then run the long way home to make it a five-mile journey. It had become my prayer path.

One day on my way home from the gym, I slowed down to a walk. I sensed God speaking to my heart. I saw a vision of men and women behind bars. Some of them were grasping the bars of the large prison cell, trying to get out. Others had given up hope and were leaning against the back walls of the prison or reclining in the shadows.

As I looked closer, I saw that they had two keys hanging around their necks. I took hold of these keys. On one key was etched *faith*. The other key said *obedience*. I placed the two keys in the lock, and then I saw a Holy Spirit explosion in my vision and the image changed. The bars that had held the prisoners captive blasted backward and became the rails of a bridge.

As I had this supernatural vision, in the natural realm I walked around a corner and there was a bridge that became one of my favorite places to pray. We call it "the bridge of breakthrough" as a family because of this vision and the encounter I had with Jesus. The Lord began to speak to my heart that *faith* and *obedience* were the foundation of the bridge of breakthrough. The rails along the side of the bridge form from the tests of trauma, struggle, and addiction we face. These tests become our testimony when Jesus transforms us.

The same obstacles that the enemy used to make you stumble in the past are today's opportunities for life-changing breakthroughs and freedom in your future.

As you begin this healing journey, ask yourself,

- *What health challenges am I facing that need God's healing?*
- *What obstacles are in my life that God wants to make an opportunity?*

One Health Challenge after Another

Have you ever had one health challenge after another? At this point in my life, I was in excellent health. One day, I ran home from the YMCA and my foot slipped off the pavement. My ankle twisted, and I fell hard. I got up feeling angry. We were about to leave for Brazil to adopt our two sons. The last thing I needed was a sprained ankle. As I walked/ran the rest of the way home, I began to do warfare prayer, resisting the enemy's attack.

While I was in Brazil my ankle recovered, but I got very sick with a fever and chills. We were there for six weeks. The First Foursquare Church in Curitiba, Brazil, *Primeira Igreja do Evangelho Quadrangular*, adopted us during our stay, welcoming us into their family. I didn't realize it then, but my gastrointestinal tract had become contaminated with parasites and rare bacterial infections. I later discovered that my compromised GI tract had triggered several autoimmune responses, including Hashimoto's thyroiditis. My body was attacking my thyroid. As a result of the low thyroid, I began to gain weight.

Initially, I was still a picture of health. When I left for Brazil, I was 125 pounds, with a muscular build. People would stop me to ask how I got such strong muscles in my arms. I was doing 100 push-ups every workout. I was a bit of a fitness fanatic, calculating the number of macronutrients per meal.

After we returned home from our travels, I remember training for a sprint triathlon and gaining unexplainable weight. Even though I was training, I had gained 20 pounds. A few days before the sprint triathlon, I got up in the morning and heard the Lord say, *You've got your father's genes; get up and fight.* My dad, who was obese, died prematurely at age 62 from cancer.

I had a urinary tract infection but pressed through to complete the triathlon after getting medicine from the doctor. Gradually, more symptoms began to show up. After throwing a large birthday party for my daughter Angela Grace, I had to go to the hospital for an emergency appendectomy. After the appendectomy, my body didn't want to recover.

I continued to gain weight, and I went to more than one doctor, trying to find out the reason. They would say that I needed to eat less and exercise more. I would pull out my journals that showed my diet and exercise records, and they would look at me as though I had a hidden habit of overeating.

Finally, after gaining weight and knowing my body wasn't doing well, I found a doctor who discovered the underlying autoimmune reactions to the contaminated GI tract. I also found a nutritionist specializing in complicated cases. By this time, I had a terrible problem of large bald spots caused by another autoimmune response called alopecia areata. My hairdresser kept my hair long and changed my part several times so that people wouldn't be able to see the problem.

We were living in a beautiful home at the time that had flooded multiple times, resulting in some mold issues. I didn't think about how it might be related then, but later I was diagnosed with CIRS, chronic inflammatory response syndrome. CIRS is a collection of symptoms caused by contamination with biotoxins. In my case, I had not only struggled with parasites and a rare chronic bacterial infection from Brazil, but also with chronic mold from my home in Tennessee. (Later, I'll share how God miraculously healed me of this and how He used me to bring healing to others.)

After a time of intense stress, including a cross-country move, my weight skyrocketed. I gained 30 pounds in two months. By this time, I was obese and stuck. I felt like a stranger in my own body.

It felt like a betrayal. I had worked out hard my entire adult life and kept track of what I was eating, but everything I used to do, which had kept me at a muscular 125 pounds, no longer worked.

Now my knees began to give me trouble. Back in my twenties, I had undergone two knee surgeries to repair my anterior cruciate ligament (ACL) and torn cartilage, but I had gone on to do triathlons in my thirties and forties. I was now in my fifties, and I had to have a double knee replacement. I inquired of the Lord, *Am I to have this surgery?*

He answered, *The miracle is in the surgery!*

Why Sickness in a Healing Book?

Why talk about sickness in a book on healing? I value authenticity. I hit a juncture in my life when it felt as though my body was falling apart. I know I'm not the only one. Like me, you may deeply believe in divine healing, yet still experience health challenges personally. I'm on a journey to encounter Jesus in the midst of this. Would you like to come on this journey with me? Let's believe together:

- That we will encounter Jesus. He's the one who heals, frees, and delivers.
- That we will gain a greater understanding of the power of God to heal body, soul, and spirit.
- That we will let go of any excuses or lies that block our ability to receive healing.
- That inner wounding of our hearts through stress, trauma, abuse, pain, or loss will be mended.
- That Jesus will deliver us from demons of infirmity and generational curses.
- That as we confess our sins to one another, we will receive healing.

I truly believe that as we focus on the healing of our inner world, our loving Father will put a ring of authority on our hands and shoes of legacy on our feet.

Called to Walk in Healing

We have a call to walk in healing, wholeness, and freedom. My mother, Donna, is 85 years old and believes it when she says out loud, "I walk in divine health!" This powerful woman increases in beauty and wisdom every year. She's joyful, full of energy, and thankful for all God is doing in her life. She has been a widow for 25 years, yet is happy and content.

What's the secret to my mom's divine health? I've thought about this a lot. She's not overweight and hasn't had the health challenges I've had. Yet Mom has eaten a bowl of ice cream before bed most of her life! She has an iron stomach and can eat anything. I've been much stricter on my diet regimen than Mom is, but I've still struggled with weight challenges. Some people struggle more with health challenges like weight gain than others. Sometimes it doesn't seem fair, and there's not always a simple answer. But here are some things I've observed about my mom that might give us some clues to her divine health:

- She declares her faith and convictions out loud: "I walk in divine health!"
- She grew up eating farm-to-table vegetables every day, and she doesn't have food sensitivities and reactions.
- She doesn't overeat, although she consistently enjoys some treats like her evening ice cream.
- She made giant choices to reduce stress at the midpoint of her life. She quit her job, even though she worked for my dad and the family business. She also dealt with her emotional pain and trauma through forgiveness.

- She embraces the boundaries she has set, and she refuses to take on stress from others.
- She has added hours of prayer, meditation, and Bible study to her daily life. She also began Bible college.
- She has traveled and enjoys her life. While at home, she enjoys the community of significant friendships she has built.

What do you do when you believe in divine healing but are personally struggling with health issues? That's also a question I have thought and prayed a lot about. Before a contaminated GI tract compromised my health, I was a bit judgmental of overweight people who seemed to have one health challenge after the other. I thought to myself, *If they would just pursue a good diet and exercise, they wouldn't be overweight.* There's some truth in that statement, but I've also realized that our bodies, minds, and spirits are more complex.

As I've discovered myself, the journey to health and wellness is a battle. I've had to wrestle with the question of why my body stopped working the way God designed it to. I was born healthy. What happened in my life that flipped a switch so that I went from being muscular and fit to being overweight and sick? Family nurse practitioner Dani Williamson's book *Wild & Well: Dani's Six Commonsense Steps to Radical Healing* helped me understand epigenetics, as well as studies on adverse childhood experiences (also called ACE).[1] Both of these have been factors for me. Epigenetics looks at how genes can be turned on or off by our life experiences. An ACE test (available many places online) looks at how various factors in our life history may have affected our health.[2]

I have a long list of exposure to biotoxins, childhood trauma, and extended periods of stress that finally flipped the switch in my body. I remember running after the DDT truck at camp, which was dispensing toxic spray to kill mosquitos. The spray filled my lungs. I also spent hours playing in moldy corn silos on the farm. When I went to Belize for three months as a young adult, I came back with open sores on my legs from botlass flies. I was also sexually abused as a child and kept this hidden. As an adult, my stress load was off the charts. And my body was keeping score of all the biotoxins, unresolved emotional pain, and trauma.

The good news is that our past does not determine our future. Just as you or I may have flipped a switch that caused us to struggle with health challenges, God is still our healer. He has designed our bodies to heal. As we cooperate with His design in our lives, our health can turn around. He is literally able to renew our youth.

Tapping into Divine Health

I'm glad to report that I have had a turning point in my health. God said to me during one encounter, *I'm giving you keys to healing chronic sickness.* (Those are the seven keys I listed for you in the introduction, and we will look at them again in chapter 5.) I embraced this word by faith in my journey of walking in divine health. I had a vision of Jesus walking with keys that opened endless doors. He handed me a large set of keys, and I knew that I needed to share these keys with the men and women in the Body of Christ who believe in divine healing but are personally experiencing health challenges.

Jesus said to me during another encounter,

> *I am beginning to heal your thyroid today! I am eradicating Hashimoto's thyroiditis, autoimmune disease, and the generational curse of your dad's family line.*
>
> *It is done! Every antibody that has attacked your thyroid is coming into alignment!*

I'm healing your metabolism supernaturally. Your gut is healed from every parasite, mold, and toxic bacteria that has hidden in your intestines.

The blood of Jesus has come. Receive My blood transfusion today! All unbelief over sickness is gone!

My daughter, you have suffered with purpose. . . . I have given you the keys to unlock and heal chronic diseases: specifically autoimmune, cancer, and unknown plagues—diseases of the blood, generational curses. You will reign with Me in healing.

Begin to write the book on healing . . . don't hold back. . . . I'm the Author and Finisher of your faith.

After I began to write *Healing Rain*, I returned to Brazil. Immediately upon arrival, I realized that I had left my thyroid medicine at home. After inquiring of the Lord and asking my intercessory team to pray, I sensed that God was completing my healing. I had received several prophecies during this trip to Brazil that Jesus was restoring everything that the devil had tried to steal from my life.

During the first week in São Paulo, I served on the ministry team of Dr. Randy Clark. I went to him, and he made it clear that doctors in Brazil could get the medication for me if I needed it. I knew all the signs of low thyroid and assured him that I would ask for help if I needed it. Then Randy and others on the team laid hands on me and prayed for complete healing.

God healed me. I served all week with divine energy flowing through me, witnessing miracles as I laid hands on the sick. As I ministered to people, they shook in the power of God. Some received inner healing and deliverance; others had a prophetic encounter with Jesus that sent them into their future.

I then traveled to Curitiba, Brazil, and preached to a ten thousand member church, *Primeira Igreja do Evangelho Quadrangular*, for most of the second week. It was a cold week for Curitiba, but I wasn't chilled. I had the energy of God to minister to the people, many nights until 1:30 a.m. because the outpouring of His Spirit was so mighty.

I returned from Brazil refreshed by God and wholly healed. Upon returning, I went to my doctor and have not needed to take thyroid medicine since. I'm so grateful.

Since the time I originally received God's prophetic word, I have slowly lost 55 pounds, and the weight loss continues. My energy levels have returned. I've tapped into divine health in my own life, and I'm sharing a few keys with you. My body has healed to the point where I can do five-mile walks with no pain and work out vigorously, lifting weights and taking classes.

I want the same breakthrough for you. You may not have had my struggle. You may be a Christian man who believes in healing, but you are dealing with prostate cancer. You may be a Christian woman who has Lyme disease or one of several autoimmune diseases. You could be young, in your twenties, and still have something like migraine headaches that plague you or allergies that make you miserable. Let's be honest with each other. Every human being alive today has experienced some type of physical setback. Everyone has had a cold or Covid or the flu. We know what it's like on this earth to experience sickness. But there is healing for you and me.

Authentic Community

I do not want to boast about sickness or meditate on disease; I want to rise and declare with my 85-year-old momma, "I walk in divine health!" At the same time, I'm not too fond of it when people feel as if they have to hide their struggles from Christian communities. It should be the opposite.

Jesus said, "It is not the healthy who need a doctor, but the sick" (Mathew 9:12 NIV). Jesus is the Great Physician who wants to walk in intimacy with you. You don't have to pretend that everything is just fine if it's not. Jesus invites you into honest dialogue and spurs you forward in faith.

Suppose you've struggled with sickness but believe in divine healing. In that case, you are in the company of giants of the faith who personally had debilitating illnesses, yet God still used them in healing ministry to others:

- *Smith Wigglesworth* regularly saw miracles in his services but suffered in agony for six years with kidney stones. Later, he suffered from sciatica that made walking painful, and often, he was sicker than the people he prayed for!

- *Aimee Semple McPherson*, who saw so many supernatural miracles, had health challenges in her fifties and died at the age of 54 of an accidental drug overdose while taking sleeping pills for insomnia.

- *Oral Roberts* nearly died of tuberculosis at age seventeen before being miraculously healed and launched into the healing ministry. He has many documented miracles from his crusades and television shows.

- *Benny Hinn*, famous for miracle crusades, has struggled with an abnormal heart rhythm called atrial fibrillation, which he has experienced intermittently for over twenty years.

Why do I mention these legendary examples? Some would point to these examples and claim that God doesn't heal today. However, the documented miracles of these four great healing evangelists show that they experienced sickness but believed in healing and miracles.

You don't have to share your struggle with everyone. You may feel God calling you to be quiet about your infirmities and boast about His goodness. However, denial of sickness may lead to more disease and suffering. You don't have to hide your struggle any longer.

Healing Moments
FOR YOUR HEART AND HEALTH

◆

As we close this first chapter, you have the opportunity to experience Jesus, your healer. Look back at this chapter and note any areas that jumped out to you personally. Now ask God this: *Are there life changes You are calling me to make?*

Write down God's response to that question in a notebook or journal. Be careful not to edit what you hear Him saying. I put His words to me in quotes. Sometimes I find myself asking Him, *How can this be?* Then I listen for His response, which is often different from my internal arguments.

After you have written down life changes both simple and big, ask God, *Are there any lies I believe about You as my healer?* Ask yourself, *Are there any lies I believe about myself or my health?* Make sure you take enough time to listen to God's voice.

When I changed from seeing myself as a victim of my circumstances, and when I disengaged from the lie that I would never be healed, I began to see gradual breakthrough. Little by little, chronic disease is under my feet. My friend, I'm praying for you to see real breakthrough in your life, too.

In a moment, I want you to pray the following prayer out loud. Before you do that, I want to acknowledge here that many in our culture have a "father wound" or a "mother wound" and sometimes bristle at calling God their Father because of the intense wounding or rejection they went through from their earthly dads or earthly moms. You may be among them. Throughout *Healing Rain* I will call you to address God as Abba, Father, or Daddy, however, because this is the primary way that Jesus talked about God. If you are feeling frustrated or far away from God as your Father, bring that out into the light and tell Him exactly how you feel. You can be honest with your emotions! Position your heart to receive healing and revelation from God about this, and again, note down whatever He shows you.

Then, pray this prayer section by section. After you've prayed through each section, listen for God's voice again and write down whatever He says to your heart.

Jesus,
I thank You that You shed
Your blood for me on the cross.
When You cried, "It is finished!"
It was a cry of triumph for my sake.

Holy Spirit,
You are my Advocate and Comforter.
You come alongside me.
You lead me and guide me.

Abba Father,
You put the lonely in a family.
You are my Papa, my Daddy.

two

R.E.S.T.

Revive Expectancy, Surrender, and Trust

I awoke one day with a clear word about R.E.S.T. The Lord said, *I want to revive expectancy, surrender, and trust in your life.* He placed it in an acronym for me:

- **R** revive
- **E** expectancy
- **S** surrender, and
- **T** trust

He then asked me to clear my schedule, which involved asking others to preach while I took a month off. He assured me that He was leading me on a pathway to restore my youthful vigor. Many times over the years, the Lord has talked to me about rest. He made it clear that Sabbath rest was holy to Him and a gift to me.

When I was physically, emotionally, spiritually, and mentally exhausted, Elizabeth Reed, a friend and functional nutritionist, said to me, "If you don't rest, you will die early. Think about working four hours a day and spending the other hours resting to rejuvenate your body, mind, soul, and spirit."

As you read this chapter, picture Jesus putting the key of rest in your hands. He's calling you to receive the gift of rest and renew your first love. Rest signifies that Jesus won back our eternal joy and healed us of our broken hearts.

Renewing First Love

Dana Candler has been part of the International House of Prayer (IHOP) for 23 years. She serves as a senior leader at the International House of Prayer in Kansas City and is also the author of *First Love: Keeping Passion for Jesus in a World Growing Cold* (Chosen Books, 2022). In a *Healing Rain* podcast interview with me, she told this story about being healed by Jesus, her first love:

> Several years ago, many of our friends and comrades were getting reassigned by the Lord to go different places. We had gotten married the first week that IHOP went 24/7, and we had built profound friendships with these people through it. I remember feeling, *How can we move forward without these precious people and families? Our hearts have been bound together in Jesus.*
>
> I felt some brokenheartedness about these people as they were moving into a different season. I had layers of the pain of loss hitting my heart at once. I remember this collision in my heart of different thoughts and emotions. I felt as if my heart weren't working anymore.
>
> In the early days, the Lord had gotten ahold of my heart, and I embraced the first commandment to *Go* after the first commandment to love God with all of my heart. I spent long hours searching for God's word to me, and deep into knowing Him I felt joy in discovering *His* beauty.
>
> I had a crisis. I knew that my heart wasn't operating as it used to. I no longer felt first love in my heart. I wanted to have

open-hearted trust. I wanted full abandonment to Jesus, without any hesitation. For a season, I spent long hours with the Lord.

I told Him, *Lord, Your Word says I am to love You with all my heart. I know You are calling me to keep my first love all my days. Your Word says that I can be fully alive.*

Jesus, something happened. I'm having trouble diagnosing the problem in my heart. I need Your grace. I need Your help.

I began a journey, with the Lord unpacking for me what went wrong. I finally began to understand by the enlightening of the Lord.

I began to see how accusation had crept in through the thoughts of my mind. The enemy doesn't come in through the front door. Many times things seep through the cracks, and we don't even know what caused the heartache.

It was a process where the Lord began to heal my heart. He touched all those places where the enemy had gotten in. It was profound. I spent lots of time in the Word and waiting on Him, saying, *Lord, You are my healer. I'm going to sit here until You heal my heart. You're the one who gives strength to the weary.*

Jesus spoke to me from Revelation 2:4, where He commended the church of Ephesus for persistence and faithfulness and then said, "I have this against you: you have abandoned your first love" [VOICE]. I felt both the confrontation of this passage, as well as the hope. I knew He was giving me the grace to do this.

Eventually, I was able to see that the accusations of the enemy had settled in my heart in the form of subtle unbelief. As I repented and returned to the Lord, He restored my passion. He called me to return to Him and do what I did at first. He met me in my place of pain when I returned to Him as my first love.[1]

Contributing Factors to Health Challenges

Have you ever found yourself depleted? If you've ever gone through a season of loss or extreme change, you may have found that your passion decreased. A downturn in the economy may have impacted you personally. Maybe you've been through the loss of a loved one or the loss of a job. You could be facing a health condition or a diagnosis that depletes your strength and energy.

Your pain could be internal, which is sometimes more challenging to share. Maybe you suffered unjust criticism, or someone you love let you down. You may have been betrayed by someone you trusted. All these things create a climate of unresolved upheaval in your life.

Maybe you feel overworked. People in helping professions like nurses, doctors, and pastors often feel that the work is so important that they need to move forward regardless of their personal challenges. We must remember that any type of work is not more important than the health and well-being of an individual.

When we don't manage stress well, we tend to accumulate it. Chronic stress raises the cortisol level in the body and has a disastrous effect on the brain. This kind of pressure is at the foundation of many types of sicknesses or health conditions,[2] including

- autoimmune diseases,
- chronic pain,
- cancer,
- cold and flu,
- depression,
- gastrointestinal disease,
- heart disease,
- memory impairment,
- obesity,
- skin conditions, and
- sleep issues.

If you face any of these challenges, I have hope for you. I believe that in our journey together through these pages, a *healing rain of revelation* will help you uproot every contributing factor to sickness and disease in your life.

Stress Impacted My Body

A year after returning home from Brazil the first time, we had a huge birthday party for our daughter Angela Grace, who was turning seventeen. After we cooked for the teenagers, we all walked across the street to the neighborhood pool. It was such a fun night, but I was exhausted by the time everyone left. By midnight everyone was sleeping, but I began vomiting nonstop. After three hours of vomiting, with extreme pain in the abdomen, I called the doctor at 3:00 a.m. and he told me to go to the emergency room.

Waking my husband up to take me to the emergency room was very difficult; he was accustomed to me being up in the middle of the night in prayer. When I woke him up, he thought I had just had a prophetic dream. My voice was calm but urgent, so he finally woke up enough to drive me to the hospital.

When I got to the hospital, the doctor said I had acute appendicitis, and they needed to operate immediately. The nurse leaned down, spoke into my ear, and compassionately said, "Honey, I know you are in intense pain. I'm going to give you a shot of morphine." I felt a tear drop down the side of my face. I was in extreme pain, and I felt so validated that someone cared about how I felt.

I'm a woman who has gone through natural childbirth many times. My daughter Rachel, trained in nursing, has told me several times, "Mom, you have an extremely high pain tolerance. You don't tend to show it on the outside, so you must let people know when you are in pain."

I had been through an entire year of chronic stress. After the appendectomy, my body didn't heal quickly. All the stress I had been under was now impacting me, and I began to experience extreme fatigue physically, emotionally, mentally, and spiritually. I didn't perceive it at the time, but I realize now that my body was giving me burnout signals.

Have You Faced Burnout?

Pastor Alejandro Morales now serves as part of Apostle Guillermo Maldonado's team at King Jesus International Ministry in Miami as the director of the Supernatural Global Network, which oversees 450 churches worldwide. The following story, which he shared with me on a *Healing Rain* podcast, is about a time in his life when he faced burnout. It happened when he was serving in ministry in Costa Rica:

> I was in the tenth year of ministry when I hit a wall. I was completely tired. I was worn out by the demands of ministry.
>
> I felt so bad, and I knew that I needed to go see a Christian psychologist. My mind, emotions, and body were in a bad state. The psychologist told me I was experiencing burnout.
>
> I was so frustrated. I went back to my office, closed the door, and began to cry. I said to God, *I preach the Gospel, I preach about Your power, I preach about Your love. I'm here! I need Your help.*
>
> God showed me that I needed to make radical changes in my life. I could not do ministry in the same way.

Later, Pastor Morales shared the following signs and symptoms of burnout in a seminar I attended.[3] See if any of them seem familiar to you.

◼ SIGNS AND SYMPTOMS OF BURNOUT

1. Extreme fatigue (physically, emotionally, mentally, spiritually)
2. Cynicism and dissociation
3. Low productivity

Pastor Morales also shared some related statistics about pastors and churches. If you are in ministry, or if you are involved in some other leadership position, you may also be familiar with some of these:

■ A FEW STATISTICS FOR PASTORS AND CHURCHES

- 38 percent of pastors are divorced or divorcing
- 21 percent spend less than fifteen minutes a day in prayer
- 38 percent of pastors considered leaving ministry after the pandemic
- 70 percent of pastors constantly fight depression
- 77 percent of pastors feel they don't have a good marriage
- 4,000 new churches are planted each year, and 7,000 churches close

A Global Reset

The shaking that began in 2020 with a global pandemic impacted everyone on the planet. Millions of people died globally. The worldwide upheaval produced a sustained emotional tension that brought many people to a breaking point emotionally, physically, mentally, and financially.

God didn't create our bodies to live in a state of prolonged stress such as the one brought on by the pandemic. Our coping abilities work best with short-term stress. Trauma from long-term stress can include the following symptoms:

- irritability
- brain fog
- confusion
- memory problems
- fear
- anxiety
- headaches
- jaw clenching
- nausea and vomiting

Any type of stress can create isolation. Catastrophes such as the pandemic lead to a loss of control that manifests in internal pain, which gives people a sense of helplessness.

Burnout Begins in the Mind

The most brutal battle is the battle within. As Paul wrote at one point in his struggles, "We were under great pressure, far beyond our ability to endure, so we despaired of life itself" (2 Corinthians 1:8 NIV).

Even under challenging circumstances, God brings good out of difficulties when we turn to Him and cry out for help. Pressure develops character. Character is not given; it is developed. Character is what builds our gift.

The internal struggle of stress takes an external toll on the body. Are you feeling burned-out or under intense pressure? Ask yourself these questions:

- Do I live a stress-filled life?
- Am I carrying heavy burdens?
- Am I experiencing financial pressure?
- Am I recovering from trauma?
- Am I stuck in patterns of addiction?
- Do I have broken relationships?
- Have I suffered from a divorce?
- Do I desire to be married, but I'm single?
- Do I desire to have children, but I haven't yet?
- Do I feel stuck or without choices?
- Have I lost my job?
- Have I been forced into a life transition?
- Have I experienced the unexpected death of a loved one?
- Have I moved recently, whether cross-country, cross-state, or even across town?
- Am I feeling extra pressure from the continuing global pandemic?

- Do I presently have unexplained health challenges?
- _____
- _____

(Fill in the blanks with other struggles you are facing.)

The trials of life can send you into a tailspin with your emotional and physical health. Too often, we try to separate our heart health from our physical well-being. Sometimes we feel as if we can't get off the treadmill of life. In those seasons, Jesus beckons us to come to Him.

A "Come to Jesus" Season

Looking back at my season, I thought I had no choice but to continue working full-time. However, I did have a choice. I could have stepped aside from my job. I could have come to Jesus for the rest of my soul. I believe that if I had made a different choice, my physical body would have been restored to total health more quickly.

Jesus speaks about the heavy burdens we tend to carry. His way is different from the world's way. Listen to His words and apply them to the life you lead and to your choices:

> Are you weary, carrying a heavy burden? Come to me. I will refresh your life, for I am your oasis. Simply join your life with mine. Learn my ways and you'll discover that I'm gentle, humble, easy to please. You will find refreshment and rest in me. For all that I require of you will be pleasant and easy to bear.
>
> Matthew 11:28–30 TPT

Take a deep breath and let these words sink into the fabric of your soul. Imagine yourself in the crowd while Jesus is preaching these words. Are you looking to your right and left and comparing yourself to others who are struggling more than you? Do you tend to deny your needs while taking care of others?

Breathe in again and imagine Jesus looking directly at you. You can't hide from His gaze. His eyes look directly into the parts of your heart and life that you tend to hide from others. He's asking *you*, "Are you weary, carrying a heavy burden?" Jesus asks this loaded, complex question that assumes your answer is yes. Then He moves forward from the question to offer you a solution to your unspoken or hidden problem. Breathe His truth into your lungs and quietly ponder His words that we just read: "Come to me . . . I will refresh your life . . . I am your oasis . . . simply join your life with mine . . . learn my ways . . . you'll discover that I'm gentle, humble, easy to please . . . you will find refreshment and rest in me . . . all that I require of you will be pleasant and easy to bear."

Whenever you begin striving, you leave His presence and provision of rest. It's no accident that the very following passage, in Matthew 12:1–2, is about the Sabbath. Let's continue with the revelation Jesus, our healer, wants to bring us today. Imagine that you are one of Jesus' disciples. You are hungry and a little tired as you walk with Him in the hot Israel sun:

> At about that time Jesus was walking through some grainfields on the Sabbath. His disciples were hungry, so they began breaking off some heads of grain and eating them. But some Pharisees saw them do it and protested, "Look, your disciples are breaking the law by harvesting grain on the Sabbath."

The disciples were not breaking biblical law as we know it. The disciples were simply not following the additional religious rules and regulations that had been added by respected rabbis of the time. Religion usually adds rules. A relationship with God calls for intimacy.

Jesus cuts through the religious expectations and comes to the heart of the issue when He says,

> But you would not have condemned my innocent disciples if you knew the meaning of this Scripture: "I want you to show mercy, not offer sacrifices." For the Son of Man is Lord, even over the Sabbath!
>
> Matthew 12:7–8

Ask yourself, *Is Jesus the Lord of my Sabbath?* Do you know that Jesus has not designed you to offer religious sacrifices constantly? Your body was not made to handle the pressure of constant stress. Every week, you've been given a gift of restoration. You've been given the gift of rest.

Embracing Jesus through the Key of Rest

One of the arguments I remember my dad and mom having regularly had to do with Sabbath rest. My dad liked to do everything fast. He valued the "American dream" mentality of hard work and pulling yourself up by your own efforts. It wasn't that my dad didn't rest. Every Sunday afternoon he snored in his chair, watching football and taking a long nap. However, Dad never took hold of the key of rest in his life. He worked as though everything depended on him. He died at 62 from cancer, his body ravaged by disease.

My mom, however, was a different story. She has embraced the Sabbath as a lifestyle. She has chosen a rhythm for her life that includes exercise, quality relationships, Bible study, and meditation. At 85, Mom looks as though she is in her sixties. She is mentally alert, physically strong, and spiritually attuned.

One of the things Mom would say to Dad when they were fighting was, "You burn the candle at both ends." What she meant was that he tended to overextend himself. He tried to do too many things in too short a time. In contrast, she conserves her energy. She builds in vacation time when she walks on the beach and listens to God's voice.

Practicing a day of rest promotes longevity. It's a biblical principle that brings emotional, mental, spiritual, and physical health. Out of the Ten Commandments, it's one that most Christians break every week.

It's vital that we each embrace Jesus as our healer through the key of rest. Then we will enjoy its benefits, which would otherwise be missing in our lives. Here are seven benefits of rest:

1. *Reduces stress*—Reducing stress is a significant benefit of Sabbath rest. Reducing stress increases health.

2. *Restores mental energy*—When you learn how to leave work at the office, it increases your mental clarity. You become more resilient in overcoming job-related stress. People who don't disconnect from their work lose balance and perspective. Sabbath rest recharges your cognitive processing abilities.

3. *Increases creativity*—A reflective time of rest helps you connect with your Creator. As you create space in your life to listen to God in unhurried ways, you open up a pathway for God's ideas. Time off will often lead to creative breakthroughs and solutions.

4. *Multiplies productivity*—Having weekly times of Sabbath rest, as well as extended sabbaticals, increases long-term productivity. It also increases your ability to maintain healthy relationships and a healthy family life, which multiplies your productivity.

5. *Increases joy*—Making time to chill and unwind with family and friends provides opportunities to make memories together doing things you love. Walking in nature, eating good food, exercising, and playing games create

opportunities to laugh. Laughter is good medicine for your heart and soul.

6. *Improves sleep*—Putting away your phone and taking a break helps remind you not to check your texts or emails right before bed. Decreasing screen time helps your body unwind. Learning to disengage from work and digital tools improves your ability to sleep deeply.

7. *Adds longevity*—Burning the candle at both ends decreases your life expectancy. Getting up early and working through the night may help you meet a deadline. However, longevity in life is increased by following God's pattern of rest.

God Rested after Creation

It only took God six days to create the world, and then He rested. He created the universe with rest for us in mind. Our crowning achievement in life is not working for God; it's allowing God to work through us. When we depend on ourselves to make things happen, we miss the multiplication and the miraculous that would benefit us when we rest.

The goodness of God carries the promise of rest. Rest sets a culture that creates the atmosphere of heaven's work to be done on earth. When we stop from our work, God works for us.

Our time on earth began with intimacy and rest. When Adam and Eve were created on the sixth day of creation, they began their time in a context of intimacy and relationship with God and each other. God breathed life into Adam face-to-face, and then said, "It is not good for the man to be alone, so I will create a companion for him, a perfectly suited partner" (Genesis 2:18 VOICE). He also walked in the Garden with Adam and gave him authority to name all the animals: "Thus the man chose names for domesticated animals, birds, and wild beasts. But none of these creatures was a right and proper partner for Adam" (verse 20 VOICE).

Then God made provision for Adam in an act of divine wisdom and goodness: "So the Eternal God put him into a deep sleep, removed a rib from his side, and closed the flesh around the opening. He formed a woman from the rib taken out of the man and presented her to him" (verses 21–22 VOICE).

Adam was so grateful to God for his companion that he said, "At last, a suitable companion, a perfect partner. Bone from my bones. Flesh from my flesh. I will call this one 'woman' as an eternal reminder that she was taken out of man" (verse 23 VOICE).

Adam and Eve celebrated intimacy with each other. They were naked and unashamed. God made man and woman in His image and blessed them with identity and destiny:

> So God did just that. He created humanity in His image, created them male and female. Then God blessed them and gave them this directive: "Be fruitful and multiply. Populate the earth. I make you trustees of My estate, so care for My creation and rule over the fish of the sea, the birds of the sky, and every creature that roams across the earth."
>
> Genesis 1:27–28 VOICE

The next day, after the wonder of their creation, Adam and Eve rested with God. Notice that Adam and Eve did not strive to get all their work done before they rested! They rested in their identity and destiny in God. They rested from God's finished work, not their own.

Striving and working to make things happen is a result of the Fall of mankind. Jesus overcame Satan's plans in the Garden of Gethsemane and restored God's original intentions and promises of the Garden of Eden.

Embracing Our Healer Begins with Rest

As new creations in Christ, we have the opportunity to live from the culture of heaven rather than the culture of earth. Your journey to embracing the full healing of your mind, emotions, spirit, and body begins with resting in the truth of God's promises of healing.

It took many years for me to turn away from my stress-filled life and begin to embrace Jesus as my healer. I consulted my nutritionist friend Elizabeth Reed, who is gifted with helping people with complicated cases of autoimmune diseases and chronic inflammation. I remember one of our first conversations, when she talked to me for an hour about rest. She made it clear that the only way forward for me in healing was through rest. I therefore made significant changes in my lifestyle:

- I changed my sleeping patterns from five to six hours of sleep a night to seven to eight hours of sleep a night.
- I embraced the Sabbath every week.
- I spent more time praying and worshiping every day.
- I put more variety into my exercise, including more stretching.
- I chose new creative work that fueled my passions.
- I ended my workday, even if the work wasn't completely done.
- I spent more time with my children and grandchildren.
- I spent more time alone with my husband.
- I increased traveling, which I enjoy.
- I invested in my passions through education, conferences, and seminars.
- I began building new life-giving friendships.

Rest has given me a testimony of health and well-being. Here are some of the results I am benefitting from:

- I can testify that this is one of my life's most creative and imaginative times.
- My mental energy and focus are restored. I look and feel younger and more vibrant. People consistently think that I'm in my late thirties or forties, and when they realize my age, they often ask me to pray over them for renewal of their youth.
- My productivity has multiplied, and I've completed my fourth book.
- Our love life has been revived, and our marriage is strong.
- I love being Mimi to our eight grandchildren and have the energy and vitality to travel internationally and nationally.
- I've had the space in my life to pursue a doctorate in ministry.
- I have the space in my mind to allow the educational process to transform me.

Healing Moments
FOR YOUR HEART AND HEALTH

◆

Rest is central to your healing, too! Ask yourself these questions:

- *Do I tend to "burn the candle at both ends"? Do I lead a hectic life?*

- *Do I get up early to get more done?*
- *Do I stay up late working on another project?*
- *Do I take 24 hours weekly to rest from work and connect with God?*

Ask the Lord to answer these questions. Listen for His voice and write down His response.

- *Lord, what does the "pace of grace" look like for this season in my life?*
- *Lord, how much sleep do I need every night to rejuvenate?*
- *Lord, what does an ideal day look like for me?*
- *Lord, what is my rhythm for days off and vacation?*
- *Lord, are there other things You want to reveal to me about rest?*

As you move into the next chapter, let's seal what we've learned about rest together in prayer. Pray this out loud:

> *God of Creation,*
> *You gave me the Sabbath as a gift and a promise.*
> *The Sabbath is not a reward for how hard I've worked.*
> *The Sabbath is a gift to rest in Your work.*
>
> *Forgive me for trying to achieve things through my efforts.*
> *Forgive me for any mindsets of unbelief.*
> *Forgive me for turning to things to try to medicate*
> *my pain.*
> *I repent of anything I have turned to other than You.*
> *I receive Your cleansing and forgiveness in faith.*
>
> *God of rest,*
> *Rejuvenate my heart with Your love.*

Renew my mind with Your Word.
Restore to me the joy of my salvation.

I pray this in the mighty name
of Jesus, Amen.

three

Heal Your Head

Transform the Way You Think

Heidi Mortenson is a licensed family and marriage therapist, and also the author of *The Brave Encourager: How the Power of Encouragement Changes the World* (Brave Publishing, 2022). In a *Healing Rain* podcast interview with me, she recounted this story about Jesus transforming the way she thinks:

> I began my healing journey when I got to the bottom of things in my marriage. We weren't communicating well. I was a licensed marriage and family therapist, but I needed help.
>
> I began to ask God more questions: *What the heck? I'm a Christian; I go to church and wear a cross around my neck. I don't feel as if I'm happy. I'm not joyful. I'm feeling depressed.*
>
> I was super confused. I got on my knees and said, *Okay, God, I don't know what to do. Show me if there is more of You. Please help me.*
>
> At that point, Jesus began to teach me from His Word. I began to search for more of Him. It was a humbling, hungry time.

I realized that I had been striving. I had been hustling for my worth. I was not doing things through the Lord. As I turned to Him, He helped me feel the unprocessed emotions and began renewing my mind.

He wanted to give me a constant renewal that revitalized my joy. My mind was being renewed in a new way. I learned He has something new for me every day.[1]

Renewing Your Mind

Just as burnout often begins in the mind, breakthrough is first conceived in the mind. Our thoughts allow burnout or breakthrough—which would you like?

The enemy has a schematic for your life. He's the god of this world. He's the god of this age. He has set in motion external temptations that open the door to demonic influence in your mind. Here is something that you can take charge of. With all of the areas in your life where you may feel as if you are losing control, your mind is the potential beginning place of absolute victory.

The mind is a powerful pathway to fullness in life. Whenever I find myself under oppression from the enemy or from some attack, I ask myself, *Do I have a door open to the enemy's attack?* Often, a back door that can allow the enemy the right of access is a doorway opened through undisciplined thoughts.

Today, you have an appointment with Jesus, your healer. He is imparting three truths to you—three choices you can make that will open doors to the supernatural realm in your life and in the lives of those whom you minister to.

1. Choose to be a victor, not a victim.

Today, make a choice not to allow your personal experience with sickness to cause you to doubt the miracles in the Bible or the blessings God wants to work through you. When I had one sickness after another plaguing my body, I began to search for medical help. My compromised health shaped a victim mentality in me as I retold my story to physicians. Unbelief seeped into my senses through unguarded thoughts like these that held partial truth:

- *I'm just getting old.*
- *I can't lose weight.*
- *Nothing I try works.*
- *I can't help my genetics from my father's side of the family.*

Instead of allowing your unguarded thoughts to give birth to unbelief, get rid of your victim mentality and embrace who you are in Christ. The Word of God anchors your soul to His truth. Declare these truths out loud so that your ears hear them:

- *I am becoming more like Jesus every day* (2 Corinthians 3:18).
- *I am created in the image of God* (Genesis 1:26–27).
- *I am a new creation in Christ* (2 Corinthians 5:17).
- *I am a joint heir with Christ* (Romans 8:17).
- *I am confident that God has begun a good work in me and will complete it* (Philippians 1:6).
- *I am holy and blameless in God's sight* (Colossians 1:22).
- *I am a partaker of God's divine nature* (2 Peter 1:4).

2. Choose to take every thought captive.

My dad used to say, "If you don't have anything good to say, don't say anything at all." He was calling us to guard the words of our mouths. I challenge you to go further and obey Paul's command to take every thought captive:

For though we walk in the flesh, we do not war according to the flesh. For the weapons of our warfare are not carnal but mighty in

God for pulling down strongholds, casting down arguments and every high thing that exalts itself against the knowledge of God, bringing every thought into captivity to the obedience of Christ.

2 Corinthians 10:3–5 NKJV

How do you take every thought captive? Ask the Holy Spirit to reveal the lies hiding in the recesses of your mind. (For more help with this, work through the "Lies I believe" versus "The truth of God's Word" exercise at the end of this chapter.)

3. Choose to speak life.

I don't know about you, but I don't want to live a life of compromise and unbelief. I want to walk in my total capacity at my age and stage. I believe that maturing in Christ is one of the most beautiful things in the world. Part of that maturing process is learning to choose to speak life.

You, too, can choose to speak life rather than death. Proverbs 18:21 (NKJV) says, "Death and life are in the power of the tongue, and those who love it will eat its fruit." If you are careful with your words, you will grow in maturity. James warns about the tongue:

Indeed, we all make many mistakes. For if we could control our tongues, we would be perfect and could also control ourselves in every other way.

We can make a large horse go wherever we want by means of a small bit in its mouth. And a small rudder makes a huge ship turn wherever the pilot chooses to go, even though the winds are strong. In the same way, the tongue is a small thing that makes grand speeches.

But a tiny spark can set a great forest on fire.

James 3:2–5

You can choose the words of your mouth. It's essential to pay attention to what words are coming out of your mouth. When I was pregnant with my first daughter, Rachel, I developed a habit of saying "I hate life" whenever something went wrong. The Holy Spirit convinced me that I was speaking a curse over the life growing inside my womb. I repented of saying these words and began to speak life over myself and my baby.

Anchor Your Hope on Jesus

Let's put all our hope in Jesus. Let's anchor our hearts on Him as our healer. Jesus came to bring life abundant. He came to pour out His lifeblood for the atonement of our sin and sickness.

Picture Jesus glorified, carrying a ring of keys.

- Keys open locked doors and treasure chests.
- Keys give you the right of access.
- Keys provide you the freedom to open passageways of opportunity.
- Keys open realms of spiritual destiny.

At the Fall of mankind, when sin entered the world, the devil grabbed these keys to the earth. Never before had humanity experienced sickness, death, or decay. At Calvary, Jesus took back these keys to death, hell, and the grave and opened a way to bring heaven to earth.

After Jesus' victory on the cross, He appeared to His disciples in resurrected form and gave them the Great Commission, saying,

> All authority has been given to Me in heaven and on earth. Go therefore and make disciples of all the nations, baptizing them in the name of the Father and of the Son and of the Holy Spirit, teaching them to observe all things that I have commanded you; and lo, I am with you always, even to the end of the age.
>
> Matthew 28:18–20 NKJV

When Jesus said, "All authority has been given to Me in heaven and on earth," He meant *all*. Sometimes when I'm teaching the Bible in a school of ministry setting, I have my students circle the word *all* every time it appears. In our human minds and reasoning, we tend to exclude concepts from the Bible that experientially we are having difficulty overcoming.

Jesus has absolute authority in heaven and on earth. The word for *authority* used in the Great Commission comes from the Greek word *exousia* and means "the authority or right to act, ability, privilege, capacity, or delegated authority."[2] Jesus had the *exousia* to forgive sin, heal sicknesses, and cast out devils. Jesus gave His followers *exousia* to preach, teach, heal, and deliver, and that authority is still available to believers today.

Healing Moments

FOR YOUR HEART AND HEALTH

❖

I recommend this exercise: Create two columns on a piece of paper. Title them "Lies I believe" and "The truth of God's Word." Dislodge and defeat the lies hiding in the recesses of your thoughts by bringing every lie into the light of God's Word. Here are some examples for you:

Lies I believe	The truth of God's Word
I'm worthless.	I have favor and a good name (Proverbs 3:3–4).
God doesn't care.	I am His treasured possession (Exodus 19:5).

Lies I believe	The truth of God's Word
I am unloved.	I am loved by God (1 John 4:9–10).
I will always suffer.	I am being restored (1 Peter 5:10).
God is far from me.	God is close to the broken-hearted (Psalm 34:18).
I have trouble.	Jesus has overcome the world (John 16:33).

Now, with the truth of God's Word planted firmly in your heart, try the following exercises to help bring even more healing into your life.

1. Pray this prayer out loud:

> *Holy Spirit, shine Your light on the*
> *hidden thoughts of my mind.*
> *Reveal thoughts that have opened*
> *the door to the enemy in my life.*
> *Show me any form of unbelief, doubt, or fear.*
> *Please help me renew my mind,*
> *making every thought obedient to Christ.*

2. Make a list of specific thoughts in your mind that have opened the door to the enemy.

3. How are you responsible for your thoughts? How do your thoughts impact your emotions?

4. Ask the Lord to show you if there have been any "triggers" that have opened the door to deceptive thoughts and disobedient actions. Write these down.

5. Ask the Lord to show you how to get rid of any obstacles so you can be fully obedient to Him. Write down anything He shows you. (For example, the Lord may have you delete some of your online streaming accounts if you have spent too much time watching things that waste your time or bring pornographic images into your home.) If He convicts you of something, take action immediately to close the door to the enemy's influence in your life.

6. Ask the Lord to remind you of His promises in your life. Close your time of reflection with thanksgiving prayers.

four

Covenant

The Promise of Health and Wholeness

Author and speaker Sherry Stahl shared this story during a *Healing Rain* podcast interview:

> I was nineteen years old; it was my first year of college. I was in excruciating pain, suffering with endometriosis. Every month, the agony returned.
>
> I regularly took heavy pain medication to function as a student. I had so many recurring cysts in my body. One cyst was so large that the doctor told me I needed surgery. She put me on medication so the cyst wouldn't rupture, warning me of the dangers if the cyst broke open before I could have the surgery. It could cause a severe infection that could lead to my death.
>
> Until they could get me into surgery, I was warned to take the medication or else I could die. As I struggled with this disease, I was at a youth event called "24 Hours for Jesus," a prayer movement for teenagers in Canada.

As thousands of teens worshiped and prayed, we took a moment to read through and declare out loud our denomination's *Statement of Faith*. My faith grew stronger as we stated who Jesus, God the Father, and the Holy Spirit are. Confidence began to rise in my heart as we declared, "I believe in divine healing."

Then I heard the Holy Spirit ask me, *Do you?*

I immediately responded, *Of course I do!* I wasn't even thinking about my situation and my need for surgery; I was just reading the words of our *Statement of Faith*.

The Holy Spirit said to me, *If you do, will you believe I can heal you so you won't need this surgery?*

I simply said, *Yes, Lord*, and I sensed the Holy Spirit prompting me to go off the medication. I realize this was a dangerous choice. Looking back, I should have told my parents and let the doctor know, but I was so filled with faith that at nineteen I took myself off the medication.

We went back to the doctor, who began discussing the surgery. When she asked me how I was feeling, I announced that I was great and told her I was no longer taking the medication because God had healed me.

The doctor looked as though she were going to have a heart attack.

So did my mom, who exclaimed, "What! You took yourself off the medicine?"

The doctor immediately sent me downstairs for an ultrasound. I became nervous and started to doubt, wondering if I'd just done a really unwise thing. After the ultrasound, I was scared while waiting on the results—partly scared of causing myself harm, but more of getting into trouble with my mom!

When I went back into the doctor's office, she looked at me and said, "I don't know how to explain this, but the cyst is gone! You don't need surgery."

I knew it was God who had touched me. He had healed me. The doctor said this condition could have taken my life, but God performed a miracle! After God miraculously healed me as a teen, I've been able to trust Him for even more physical healings.[1]

God's Nature Is to Heal Us

The healing power of God is who He is. One of the names of God revealed in Exodus 15:26 is that He is Yahweh Rapha, the God who heals. He made a healing covenant in this Scripture, where He said,

> If you will listen carefully to the voice of the LORD your God and do what is right in his sight, obeying his commands and keeping all his decrees, then I will not make you suffer any of the diseases I sent on the Egyptians; for I am the LORD who heals you.

Healing is not just something God does; it's who He is. God is your healer. You don't have to beg God to heal you; it's already His character to heal. His nature is to heal you.

The Hebrew word for heal is *rapha* and means "to cure, to heal, to repair, to mend, to restore." God is about bringing healing in the broadest sense. One of my favorite passages to pray out loud on healing is Psalm 103:1–5:

> Let all that I am praise the LORD; with my whole heart, I will praise his holy name. Let all that I am praise the LORD; may I never forget the good things he does for me. He forgives all my sins and heals all my diseases. He redeems me from death and crowns me with love and tender mercies. He fills my life with good things. My youth is renewed like the eagle's!

God heals us through forgiveness. He redeems things in our lives that have died. He even restores our youth like the eagle's. Eagles like to fly high above the earth. When an eagle needs healing, it will fly to a safe sanctuary, where its old feathers will be discarded and new feathers will grow in their place. An eagle's youth being restored is a picture for us of God's healing in our lives.

Bringing Heaven's Healing to Earth

There are no sick people in heaven. All disease is gone, and believers inherit heavenly bodies. Jesus brought heaven's reality of
healing to earth. He demonstrated the Kingdom advancing by
healing the sick and casting out demons, and He calls His disciples to do the same.

When Jesus and His disciples came down from the moun-
tain one day, they stood on a large, level area and were soon
surrounded by many of His followers and the crowds (see Luke
6:12–19). There were people from all over Judea and Jerusalem and
as far north as the seacoasts of Tyre and Sidon. They had come
to hear Him and to be healed of their diseases. Those troubled by
evil spirits were also healed. Everyone was trying to touch Jesus
because healing power went out from Him. Healing power from
heaven was flowing through Him, and everyone who touched
Him was healed.

Jesus had a way of shaking up the status quo. Another day, He
went across the lake from Galilee to the region of the Gerasenes.
A demon-possessed man came running to meet Him before He
got out of the boat (see Luke 8:26–39). This man was homeless,
naked, and living in the graveyard outside town. The people were
terrified of this man and would sometimes put him in chains,
which he would break with the strength of the legion of demons
controlling him. Jesus sent the legion of demons into a herd of
pigs.

The people rushed out to see what had happened and were
surprised to see the fully clothed, no longer demonized man in
his right mind, sitting at Jesus' feet. They were filled with fear:
"Then those who had seen what happened told the others how
the demon-possessed man had been healed. And all the people
in the region of the Gerasenes begged Jesus to go away and leave
them alone, for a great wave of fear swept over them" (verses

36–37). The Greek word *sozo*, which describes this man's healing in Luke 8, is a comprehensive word that means:

1. *To save, saved, salvation*—The New Testament uses the Greek word *sozo* over a hundred times. It's an all-encompassing word for salvation.
2. *Forgiven, healed, and delivered*—The word *sozo* is translated 53 times as "saved" (past tense) regarding forgiveness of sins. However, there are also times when this same Greek word is translated as "healed." This same word that's used for both forgiveness of sins and physical healing also applies to deliverance.
3. *Made whole*—This same word, *sozo*, is also translated as "made whole" regarding healing. Consider the example of the woman with an issue of blood (see Luke 8:43–48).
4. *Abundantly supplied*—Salvation doesn't only mean forgiveness of sins, but also includes healing of the body, deliverance, and financial prosperity. God has provided *everything* we need in this life and in the future—forgiveness of sins, healing, deliverance, and prosperity. Isn't God good?!

Do You Believe in Divine Healing?

In every circumstance where there's a need for physical healing, do you immediately turn to God and ask for healing? Or do you tend to research the problem and turn to medical help first? In North America, many Christians go to the doctor first and ask for prayer later.

I want to approach healing and miracles differently. I want to put Jesus first in every area of my life, including anchoring my faith on Him as my healer.

One Sunday morning several years ago, when I was serving as an associate pastor, I saw a picture of a uterus with dark nodules and cysts. I knew that the enemy was attacking someone in the church with endometriosis. As I gave a call for healing, one woman began to weep, knowing that I was giving a word of knowledge about her condition. A few years earlier, she had given birth to a stillborn child. Going through the trauma of birthing her stillborn baby had not only wounded her heart, but had also left scars on her soul.

After the service, a number of women gathered in a circle with me to pray for healing. God prophetically spoke about how the enemy had tried to prevent life from growing inside them. After we prayed for complete healing and spoke life, most of the women in the circle (but not me) got pregnant right away. Nine months later, most of us had new children—the women in the circle had babies, and Wayne and I had adopted our sons from Brazil. We laughed at the overflow of God's blessing.

I've seen hundreds of babies born after I've prayed for people with infertility issues. Sometimes, I prayed prayers of healing within the church community. Other times, I met people outside the church and prayed for them. It became a joke that "you don't want to ask Pastor Sue to pray unless you want to get pregnant."

It's Easier to Pray for Others

Is it easier to pray for someone else's healing than for your own? I'm full of faith in praying for others, but I'm more likely to fall into doubt when I have to deal with my own daily symptoms. How about you?

I was born with a mitral valve prolapse. When I was in college, a doctor monitored it because I was an athlete. A couple of years ago, I failed a heart stress test. After having an electrocardiogram, I went in for an echo stress test, which used an imaging machine to look at my heart.

The stress test was suddenly stopped, however, and the doctor looked at me solemnly. "We need to schedule you for surgery," I was told. "We have to do a coronary angiogram, where we inject dye into your body to look at the blood vessels of your heart. In the meantime, here's a prescription for you to carry medication. Keep it with you at all times!"

When the doctor warned me that this was a life-and-death situation, the breath went out of me. I thought, *I'm too young to face this!* A few years earlier, during seminary, I had served as a chaplain in the hospital and had spent much time with heart patients on the cardiac floor. I remember fit men in their late thirties and forties being shocked at being in the hospital and undergoing these procedures. It was much easier believing and praying with them than facing the same kind of prognosis myself.

Broken Heart Syndrome

God miraculously healed my heart. A few weeks after that sobering doctor appointment, I was praying and worshiping in my room when I sensed God's presence. Heat flowed from the top of my head like hot oil down to my feet. My heart was burning with His presence as He miraculously healed me. I was shaking all over, and His joy touched my heart.

He spoke this to me in that encounter: *I'm not only healing your physical heart, but I'm also healing your broken heart.*

I knew what He meant. As I encountered Jesus as my healer, soaking in His presence, He brought my recent loss to mind. He was healing my broken heart from the sorrow of losing my son, Dre. (I'll tell you more about Dre's story in chapter 6.) I had a small "healing team" of people whom I had been talking to after the loss of my son, including a professional counselor. Yet until that healing encounter I had with Jesus, I had not connected the physical heart issue I was facing with the emotional loss of my son.

After my encounter with Jesus, all my physical heart symptoms ceased. I went through with the coronary angiogram for the sake of my husband and children, who were concerned about me. I knew already, however, that my heart had been completely healed. The angiogram confirmed it.

Later, I interviewed international speaker and minister Joan Hunter on my *Healing Rain* podcast and learned about broken heart syndrome. Extreme situations of emotional stress or heartache can bring on temporary physical heart conditions. Walking in the supernatural does not always prevent you from personally experiencing trials and difficulties on this earth. Joan related her experience with this syndrome:

> I had broken heart syndrome. Some people have a broken heart because of difficult situations with their children, spouse, or ministry. Having a broken heart can kill you. I talk about it in my book *Love Again, Live Again*.[2] I was healed, and now I have no symptoms.
>
> I married my first husband when I was twenty. We traveled internationally with my parents, Charles and Francis Hunter, and saw many miracles. I co-pastored with my husband for eighteen years in the Dallas area. However, on the side, my ex-husband was living a double life. After being married for 25 years and knowing about his adulterous homosexual affairs for 12 years, I stood and believed for him to recognize that what he was doing was a sin and for our marriage to be restored. I fought for our marriage for years, till I heard the Lord say, *You are free to go.*
>
> My heart was broken; I was divorcing a man whom I still loved. When the children became aware that their dad was living a gay lifestyle, it was a difficult time for all of us. Two days after our divorce, I found out I had breast cancer. The doctors gave me two years to live.
>
> I went after getting my heart healed. I can live without a breast, but I can't live with a broken heart. I went after getting rid of the worry, the trauma, the unforgiveness, the betrayal, and abandonment. When I got the emotions of my heart healed, then I went back to the oncologist, and they couldn't find cancer! They asked me, "What did you do with the cancer?" I said, "I sent it home to hell, where it belongs."

Around the same time of all this trauma, my doctor diagnosed me with broken heart syndrome. I couldn't breathe; I had so many heart symptoms. When I received emotional healing, I no longer had any physical symptoms of a heart condition.[3]

Recognizing how closely related physical and spiritual symptoms are, ask yourself these questions:

- *What areas of emotional pain and loss are presently impacting my physical issues?*
- *Do I tend to ignore dealing with emotional issues and just try to move on with life?*
- *Are there areas of unresolved mental anguish, bitterness, or grief that are affecting my body?*

Declarations of Faith

One of the ways to lessen the gap between believing in healing and experiencing healing is to declare truths based on Scripture. Isn't it amazing that nineteen-year-old Sherry Stahl was healed as she claimed a statement of faith? I want to give you an opportunity to stand up and say out loud some foundational beliefs from the Gospel.

Are you ready? Get in a place where you are not self-conscious about speaking out loud the truth of God's Word. Be willing to let your voice rise as faith fills your heart. You can use the following declarations daily, like taking medicine for your heart and body. (If these declarations are new to you, take time to read each Scripture listed in them.)

1. I believe in the atoning work of Jesus Christ, who died on the cross for me and took my sin. I receive salvation by faith, through grace, when I repent of my sin and make Jesus the Lord and Savior of my life. Salvation is God's

gift to me. While I was still a sinner, Jesus died for me and pardoned me. (John 3:16; Romans 5:8; Ephesians 2:8)

2. As I confess and repent of my sin, Jesus is faithful to forgive me of my sin and cleanse me of all unrighteousness. I am justified not by my works, but by a gift from God. (Romans 10:8–10; 1 John 1:9)

3. I believe that genuine transformation occurs when I embrace Jesus as my Savior. My old life passes away, and the new comes as I allow Christ's life to be lived through me. (2 Corinthians 5:17; Galatians 2:20)

4. I believe it is God's will that I daily walk in the power of the Holy Spirit. I believe the Holy Spirit continues to give spiritual gifts to believers. I believe that the fruit of the Holy Spirit can be active in my daily life. (Galatians 5:22–25; 1 Corinthians 12:4–11)

5. I believe the Bible is God's inspired Word. I nourish my spirit, soul, and body every time I read and meditate on the Word of God. (2 Timothy 3:16–17)

6. I believe that hell is an eternal place of torment separated from God's love, and that heaven has been prepared for me as a glorious eternal home. I believe that as a believer, I am called to share the good news of the Gospel with others and invite them to receive Jesus as their Lord and Savior, and to make disciples. (Matthew 28:19–20; Mark 16:15; John 14:1–3; Revelation 7:15–17; 20:11–15)

7. I believe I am called to continue to grow in my walk with Jesus, be sanctified, and grow in faith. I embrace being part of the global and local Body of Christ, and I embrace fellowship with other believers. I embrace visible signs of my covenant through baptism in water and through regularly commemorating the Lord's Supper. (Mathew 28:19; Romans 6:4; 1 Corinthians 11:24–25; Hebrews 6:1; 10:24–25)

8. I believe baptism with the Holy Spirit empowers me to walk in the fullness of God's plan for my life. I believe in divine healing. I believe Jesus has given us power to heal the sick in answer to prayers of faith. (Acts 2:1–4; Mark 16:15–18; James 5:14–16)

My friend, I pray that God will build a strong foundation of faith in your life. I pray that you will declare out loud your faith in the one who is the healer of your body, mind, soul, and spirit.

Healing Moments
FOR YOUR HEART AND HEALTH

◆

Answer the following questions in your notebook or journal as you reflect on what you've read in this chapter.

- Are you ready to stand up and fight for your healing? If not, what's holding you back?
- As you read Joan Hunter's words about broken heart syndrome, did you think of heart issues related to any physical sickness you face?
- Make two columns, and on one side of the page list your heart issues. On the other side, list your physical symptoms. Here is an example:

    Heart Issues   *Physical Symptoms*
    worry   sleeplessness

- Do you have head knowledge where you believe in divine healing more than you actually experience divine healing? If so, what are some ways to lessen the gap between your head knowledge and your divine healing experience?

- Is it easier for you to pray with faith for others than to believe in faith for yourself? If so, how can you more actively stand, pray, and believe in your own healing?

five

Gateway

Experiencing the Power of Communion

While I was beginning this chapter on the power of Communion, our third daughter, Hannah, who was in the first trimester of her third pregnancy, began spotting. She had already suffered a miscarriage during her first pregnancy. As the bleeding became profuse, she felt 95 percent sure she was miscarrying again.

I began to carry the weight of this trial in prayer. All through the night, I struggled in and out of sleep. I woke up and took Communion with my husband, and we prayed in faith for Hannah and the life and destiny of our eighth grandchild. We prayed in agreement for God's protection.

I received this text from Hannah when she and her husband were with the midwife:

Baby is GOOD!! The heartbeat is strong; the baby is measuring the correct size. The midwife thinks the bleeding is a subchorionic hemorrhage they missed at my last ultrasound.

I'm weeping as I finalize this chapter later, and praising God. I believe we experienced a miracle on behalf of our eighth grandchild, Jonathan Allen, born healthy and whole. I'm crying with thanksgiving for the signs and wonders Jesus has done on behalf of our family. And just as God healed our grandson while he was in his mother's womb, God is going to bring healing to your life and family as well. His blessings are eternal. He is in the details of our lives. His goodness never ends.

After this miracle of healing, I began to take Communion every day as part of my prayer time. Sometimes I use the written prayers at the end of this chapter to meditate on all Jesus has done for me. Usually, I lift the bread and the cup, and I use it as a time to pray for our children, grandchildren, and anyone else who comes to my mind who needs physical healing.

As you read this chapter, think about ways to incorporate Communion into your personal and family times. My husband, Wayne, and I regularly take Communion together when praying and believing for specific promises of God to be fulfilled in our lives.

The Power of Communion

Communion was a big deal when I was growing up, but we only took it twice a year. We included a love feast and foot washing as part of our remembrance of what Jesus did. I'm grateful for the beauty and power of corporate Communion.

Jesus' shed blood overcomes every manner of sickness and disease in my life. Faith fills my heart every morning as I lift up the bread and the wine and take it like medicine during my personal times of worship and prayer. We also began to take Communion during our monthly encounter group that has met in our home. We have seen so many healings and miracles.

The Lord's Supper is much more than a religious ritual to me. As a reminder of everything Jesus did for me on the cross, it is a gateway to health and healing. As part of my daily prayer time, I take a moment to remember Jesus' body and acknowledge the mental, physical, emotional, and spiritual anguish Jesus overcame.

When I drink the cup, I remember that Jesus delivered me from every curse, temptation, addiction, anxiety, poverty, fear, sickness, and disease. I meditate on the seven places where Jesus bled from His body and the seven keys that unlock divine health for me. (For more on these and how they are related, I encourage you to watch my video teaching called "7 Keys to Divine Health."[1]) I listed the seven keys for you in the introduction, but now look at them again with Communion in mind:

> *The key of freedom* gives you the authority to make good choices with your will.
>
> *The key of connection* opens the door to right standing with God.
>
> *The key of health* gives you victory over your physical infirmities.
>
> *The key of prosperity* brings you victory over mental torment and physical poverty.
>
> *The key of influence* gives you authority over every area of your life, home, and work.
>
> *The key of purity* gives you victory over your internal pain and suffering.
>
> *The key of rest* signifies that Jesus won back our eternal joy and healed us of our broken hearts.

Again, the Lord's Supper helps us remember everything Jesus did for us on the cross. When you eat the bread, which represents Jesus' body, and when you drink the cup, which represents His blood, you acknowledge the mental, physical, emotional, and spiritual anguish Jesus overcame to deliver you from every curse, temptation, addiction, anxiety, poverty, fear, sickness, and disease.

DIVING DEEPER
IN GOD'S WORD

Let's begin to experience the power of Communion by following in the steps of Jesus. Stop and take a moment to do a deep dive with Him, studying the Word of God and applying it to your life.

Read Luke 22:7–20. What was Jesus establishing for His disciples as He prepared them for His crucifixion?

Read Luke 22:39–46. Describe how Jesus overcame temptation in the Garden of Gethsemane. How did His response to temptation differ from the disciples' response?

Read Luke 22:54–62. Has there been a time when you denied Jesus, as Peter did?

Overcoming Suffering and Loss

My father made such an impact on my life. He was an entrepreneur who owned six corporations. Dad used farming as a tax write-off, but he loved getting on a tractor himself. He was a very earthy man, and farming was fun for him. As a builder, he would often stop at a construction site, then arrive home tracking in mud. One time when he came home with dirty shoes, he found that the governor had come to lunch! But that was all right because he was unconcerned about how he looked to people. I grew up understanding the urgency of the harvest. I loved riding on top of the wagons, harvesting grain, when I was young. I also loved riding the tractor beside my dad, until one day when I was six the tractor wheel hit a hole and I flew off and was knocked unconscious.

My mom was in the car with packed lunches for the workers and saw the accident. I had a few bruises and burns from the hot metal of the tractor, but the main consequence was that I was no longer allowed to ride the tractor with Dad. My three older brothers and cousins were the ones who worked through the night to bring the harvest in every year.

When my dad died suddenly at the age of 62 from cancer, I went with my 59-year-old mom to pick out his gravestone. We walked across from my dad's busy downtown company headquarters for building and real estate, into the stone engraver's storefront. Immediately, we saw a beautiful grey slate headstone carved with grains of wheat. Mom and I both began to cry and hug each other. We knew it was perfect for this earthy man who had impacted a region for good.

My dad was an apostle in the marketplace. He had a prophetic gift of giving that is rare in the Body of Christ. He knew what you needed before you did. Dad was a harvester. One of the Scriptures we chose for his gravestone was John 12:23. Let's take a moment to look at it more closely.

DIVING DEEPER
IN GOD'S WORD

Take another deep dive into the Word by reading the following Scripture passage. As you read it, circle, underline, or highlight what stands out to you.

Jesus (to Philip and Andrew): The time has come for the Son of Man to be glorified. I tell you the truth: unless a grain of wheat is planted in the ground and dies, it remains a solitary seed. But when it is planted, it produces in death a great harvest. The one who loves this life will lose it, and the one who despises it in this world will have life forevermore. Anyone who serves Me must follow My path; anyone who serves Me will want to be where I am, and he will be honored by the Father.

John 12:23–26 (VOICE)

Now go back through this passage and list in two columns on a piece of paper the phrases that describe these two concepts: *dying* and *harvesting*. (If you need more room, grab your notebook.) Here is one example:

Dying	*Harvesting*
Being planted	Being productive

Jesus Is the Passover Lamb

Every milestone in Jesus' life happened on a Jewish holiday.[2] Jesus' death on the cross happened during Passover. He's known as the Passover Lamb. Passover commemorates the liberation of the Jewish people from the oppression of Egypt through God's miraculous intervention. We all have our own personal "Egypt," which represents places in our lives where we've been held captive. What God did when He delivered His enslaved people, the Israelites, from Egypt He can do for you today.

The Last Supper that Jesus celebrated with His disciples is the Last Seder. The highlight of Passover is this meal, which is usually eaten at home with friends and family. They would eat together a flat, cracker-like bread called matzah that represents freedom and healing, remembering how God freed them from Egypt's oppression.

During the Last Seder, Jesus would have taken four cups, representing the four promises God gave of redemption:

1. The first cup is known as the "Cup of Sanctification," remembering God's promise to make His people holy and set apart.
2. The second cup is known as the "Cup of Deliverance," remembering the signs and wonders God did through the ten plagues.
3. The third cup is known as the "Cup of Redemption," remembering the blood of the Passover lamb that was put over the doorposts. We remember the shed blood of Jesus, who is our perfect Passover Lamb.
4. The fourth cup is known as the "Cup of Thanksgiving," which looks to the future as we look forward to drinking this cup at the final Marriage Supper of the Lamb.

We can remember the perfect sacrifice of Jesus every time we take Communion. Like the Passover lamb of Seder, Jesus delivers us out of our places of tight confinement. He overcomes the "pharaohs" in our lives that rob us of identity and destiny.

Healing Moments
FOR YOUR HEART AND HEALTH

Answer these questions on paper, describing in your own words the process of dying that Jesus calls us to:

1. Why does God call us to die?
2. Is there an area in your life He's calling you to surrender or lay down in this season?
3. What does Jesus promise if you die to yourself?
4. How does the concept of self-denial impact your health?

The significance of understanding the Last Supper in light of the Last Seder involves doing these three things:

1. Look back and remember the miracles God has done in your past. Take a moment to write about the past miracles Jesus has done for you. Fill your notebook with thanksgiving.
2. Next, honestly assess whether there are areas in your life where you presently need greater freedom. Believe that God will free you from any captivity you presently struggle with. Ask Jesus in faith for your deliverance.

3. Now fearlessly look forward in faith because of who God has shown Himself to be. Look forward to the things Jesus is calling you to step into in faith. Write out a prayer thanking Him for who He is and praising Him for what He will do in the future.

While you are writing these things down, make it a conversation with Jesus. Take some moments to listen to His voice. Write down what you hear Him saying to you. If you feel led, take Communion personally.

Communion

The Lord has prepared a table for us that points toward His Second Coming every time we partake of it. Lift the bread and hold it up. Think about how you are holding up the body of Christ. Pray these prayers out loud, either when taking Communion as a group or taking it individually:

Prayer over the Bread

Jesus, I humbly come to Your table with thanksgiving for all You've accomplished. I thank You for this bread that represents Your body. Thank You for overcoming sin, temptation, addiction, anxiety, poverty, fear, sickness, and disease. Your body took on what I could not bear. Thank You that Your body took on my sorrow, guilt, and condemnation.

Today as I eat the bread, I boldly proclaim Your Word: "I have been crucified with Christ and I no longer live, but Christ lives in me. The life I now live in the body, I live by faith in the Son of God, who loved me and gave himself for me" [Galatians 2:20 NIV].

I receive total healing in my body, soul, and spirit as I eat the bread. Thank You for Your total provision for every need I have today. Thank You that as I eat this bread, I am proclaiming my unity with the rest of the Body of Christ around the world.

Jesus, I thank You that Your broken body mends every broken relationship in my life. I receive Your forgiveness for every sin I've committed against those You have created and love. I take this bread and proclaim Your salvation and deliverance over every covenantal relationship in my life [mention the needs of those you love at this point: spouse or future spouse, children, grandchildren, friends]. Thank You for Your body broken for us.

Eat the bread in faith. Then, as you lift the cup, allow wonder to awaken your heart to what you are holding. See it as the blood of Jesus shed on the cross.

Prayer over the Cup

Father, thank You that in Leviticus 17:11 [NKJV], Your Word says, "For the life of the flesh is in the blood, and I have given it to you upon the altar to make atonement for your souls; for it is the blood that makes atonement for the soul." Father, thank You for providing Your Son, Jesus, as my Passover Lamb. As I hold this cup of sanctification, I remember Your promise to make Your people holy and set apart.

Jesus, thank You for becoming my Sacrificial Lamb. As I hold this cup of deliverance, I'm in awe of the transformational provision You have placed in this cup. It's more powerful than any medicine I could take or any food I could eat. It is Your blood shed for me. Your blood is more powerful than any attack against my family or me through curses, genetics, viruses, diseases, or plagues.

Jesus, thank You for the cup of redemption that deals with every form of sin in my life and ultimately in this world. Jesus, Your blood was shed over seven areas of Your body, each giving me a key to divine health and healing. Your wounds provide for every type of mental, physical, and spiritual anguish, all of which You overcame on the cross. Thank You that Your blood calls me to be in intimate companionship with You and the rest of Your Bride. Thank You for paying the price for my past, present, and future sins.

Holy Spirit, be present with me right now as I drink the cup of thanksgiving. Thank You, Jesus, that every evil assignment against my family and me was made powerless by the shedding of Your blood. I thank You that I have a far better future than I could ever hope for without Your blood. As I take this cup of thanksgiving, I celebrate how one day soon, I will be drinking this cup with You and the others in Your Body at the final Marriage Supper of the Lamb. In Your name, Amen.

Now drink the cup as wonder fills your heart! Let the gateway of Communion once again remind you of the freedom, health, and wholeness Jesus has purchased on the cross for us.

six

A Troubled Heart

The Trap of Disappointment, Sorrow, and Loss

"Are you the mother of Alexandre Joel?"

"Yes, I am."

"I'm a coroner. I regret to tell you that I have your son. He died of an apparent drug overdose."

Jesus, help me, I prayed as I sobbed. "Can I come to see him?"

"He's already been identified. I don't recommend that you come to see him. It would be best if you remembered him alive. It was a cold night last night, and there may be hypothermia. I will do an autopsy to determine the cause of his death."

The coroner's voice on the long-distance phone call was kind and gentle. I thought of my 23-year-old son, a tall, black Brazilian man, lying cold in the morgue.

Then I saw a picture of my son Dre (Alexandre Joel) in my mind. His big smile lit up the room. There was an innocence about Dre, and a deep love for Jesus. I thought of him as a twelve-year-old little boy in a green-and-yellow shirt that reminded me of the Brazilian flag. He was standing awkwardly next to my husband. His brother, Ezequiel Paul (Zeke), was already on my lap. In the Brazilian village of Jardim Allegra (Happy Garden), we talked to a Brazilian judge. Our large family had traveled at great expense to adopt these two boys.

"I love you, Mom and Dad," Dre said with a big smile. I could tell he had practiced those words to communicate them in English.

"*Eu te amo*," I said. My smile matched his as tears fell down my cheek. The tension broke with these words, and Dre seemed to relax. I hugged Zeke as he sat on my lap. He arched his back and giggled. After being found on the street numerous times in their young lives, the boys had grown up in an orphanage. They were both born addicted to the drugs and alcohol taken by their biological mother.

The kind, gentle voice of the coroner continued to speak. I was no longer comprehending his words as shock flooded my emotions. I could feel cortisol and adrenaline pumping through my body as I plunged into deep grief. A few days before, we had received news of my husband's mom dying, and we were already preparing to travel as a family for one funeral.

When God had called our family to adopt Dre and Zeke from Brazil, we had not imagined this early death. We were pastors who already had four beautiful biological daughters, ages eighteen, sixteen, fourteen, and twelve. God broke our hearts for the plight of older orphans who became street kids in Brazil and often experienced violence and abuse.

"It will take six weeks for the autopsy results to be complete," the coroner said. My spinning head and heart returned to what he was telling me.

I said quietly through my sobs, "Thank you for letting me know."

I called my husband at work, and he prayed for me. We agreed that I should call Zeke, who lived in Austin, Texas.

Zeke and I sobbed for fifteen minutes over the phone. "Mom, Dre always helped me. What am I going to do now?"

As we talked with each member of our large family, we agreed to travel cross-country to Grammy's funeral first. Then we would delay Dre's memorial service until everyone could be together again.

"Mom, I saw heaven," Zeke said two days later. "It was as if I floated above the earth, and I was in a beautiful place. The light was so bright, and the colors were so beautiful. The grass was so green. I was happy walking along, and I heard Dre's voice say, 'I'm all right, bro. I'm in heaven.' He smiled at me. I felt so much peace. Heaven is such a real place."

"That's amazing, Zeke." I felt a heaviness fall off me as I thought about Dre in heaven. "He loved Jesus. I know Dre is with Him now." We were both comforted.

"Mom, I sense God calling me to get my life straight. I owe it to my brother to live my life right," Zeke said.

Healing the Heart

The heart is at the center of our need for healing.[1] One of the difficult things about death is its finality on this earth. We feel the searing loss of not being able to spend time with the one we lost. There are no more conversations, no more Thanksgivings, no more Christmas celebrations, no more birthday parties with the one who died.

We tend to run from our pain rather than wait on Jesus to heal our hearts. Unhealed trauma in our hearts provides a feeding frenzy for the demonic realm. Whenever our pain exceeds our joy, we are open to the enemy's attacks.

Even tiny traumas can paralyze you and hold you back from the fullness of joy that is your inheritance. The enemy knows where you are most vulnerable. He feasts on wounded flesh. When your soul (your mind, will, and emotions) is not at peace, it is a heart issue. Jesus is the only one who can completely heal a wounded heart. Hearts that are truly connected to Jesus are intuitively free.

Our hearts are complex. Jesus is the only one who can go to the root issues in our lives. Often, our hearts retain repressed memories of early pain. If we follow the symptoms of pain in our lives back to the original trauma, Jesus sets us free at the source of the pain. Unresolved trauma keeps us from freedom. It's easy to believe lies and hold on to anger. It's more difficult and tender to become like a child and bring our bumps and bruises to Father God.

The center of your spiritual life is your heart. When the Bible talks about the heart, it talks about the essence of who we are. To be wholehearted is to be fully connected to Jesus and at peace. Jesus relentlessly pursues our hearts.

The heart is the starting place for healing. God knows our hearts, even when we don't. He wants us to desire what He wants. Every addiction is born out of unhealed trauma. Addiction is a way for us to run away from or medicate our pain.

The word for *heart* in Hebrew is *lev*, but it does not refer to the physical organ in our bodies. The Israelites had a broader concept of the heart that meant the inner essence or center of your being. They did not have a concept of the brain or have any word for it. They believed that intellectual thinking and reasoning were performed in the heart. Contemplate these phrases, drawn from the many and various verses in the Bible about the heart:

- *Know* with your *heart.*
- *Wisdom* dwells in the *heart.*
- *Discern* truth and error with your *heart.*

The heart in the Bible is where you process your emotions. According to Hebrew thought, you can experience fear, depression, and distress in your heart. You can also experience feelings of joy or happiness in your heart.

The Hebrews also saw the heart as the place where you make choices. Your heart is what carries your hidden motivations or "secrets of the heart." Your true heart's desire is seen clearly by God, but is sometimes hidden from you and others. The heart is the center of human existence.

Proverbs 4:23 says, "Guard your heart above all else, for it determines the course of your life." Your heart is the guiding center for the decisions that you make according to a system of beliefs. Strongholds in our thoughts are connected to what we have accepted to be true. The heart controls the core ideology and is an anchor point for our perceived reality and relationships. What we believe to be true becomes a navigating structure for how we live our lives. What you hold to be true in your heart oversees your thought process and your behavior.

The hope for healing is found in a renewed heart. After David committed adultery with Bathsheba, he pleaded with God: "Keep creating in me a clean heart. Fill me with pure thoughts and holy desires, ready to please you" (Psalm 51:10 TPT).

Years of wrong choices, evil desires, addictions, and hidden sins can take a toll on your heart. Ezekiel prophesied to his generation, which had been held in captivity because of their sin. He knew that only God Himself could heal the trauma they had experienced. God's promise to His people comes through these words:

> I will sprinkle you with clean water, and you will be clean. I will wash away all of your dirtiness, and you will be clean and pure, free from the taint of idols. I will plant a new heart and new spirit inside of you. I will take out your stubborn, stony heart and give

you a willing, tender heart of flesh. And I will put My Spirit inside of you and inspire you to live by My statutes and follow My laws.

Ezekiel 36:25–27 VOICE

Daily cleansing from sin was a Jewish practice. Daily, the Israelites were called to pray the Shema. Every day, the Jewish people were called to give their hearts to God. In Jewish thought, this would be dedicating their whole being to God—their thoughts, emotions, desires, dreams, and future, and their failures, sins, and traumas. As a Jewish man, Jesus would have grown up praying the Shema every day:

Hear, O Israel: The LORD our God, the LORD is one! You shall love the LORD your God with all your heart, with all your soul, and with all your strength.
    And these words which I command you today shall be in your heart.

Deuteronomy 6:4–6 NKJV

Look how The Voice translation words this passage:

Listen, Israel! The Eternal is our True God—He alone. You should love Him, your True God, with all your heart and soul, with every ounce of your strength. Make the things I'm commanding you today part of who you are.

Jesus our High Priest did the true cleansing of our hearts. He brought heaven to earth. The Tabernacle was a model of heaven, but Jesus brought the real thing through His presence. Jesus' covenant is one of grace, brought to the hearts and minds of believers by the power of the Holy Spirit. No longer is God's relationship with His people based on external reality; it is now an impelling power from within:

But this is the new covenant I will make with the people of Israel on that day, says the LORD: I will put my laws in their minds, and I will write them on their hearts. I will be their God, and they will be my people.

Hebrews 8:10

The Trap of a Troubled Heart[2]

Believing in God is the beginning of true heart health. In the Upper Room Discourse (see John 13–17), Jesus knew the disciples were about to go through their biggest heart challenge. As He prepared them for His death, He said, "Don't let your hearts be troubled. Trust in God, and trust also in me" (John 14:1).

The Greek word for *troubled* in John 14:1 is *tarassestho*, which means "to agitate, stir up, disturb." In the New Testament, the word *troubled* is used metaphorically to describe the mental anguish or fear you face when your world is turned upside down. A troubled heart can bring anxious or distressing thoughts or doubt.

Jesus knew that the disciples were going to go through the toughest test of their lives when He faced the cross. Like a good leader, He set up His friends and comrades for success. He gave them the key to overcoming the temptation they were about to face. The key was keeping their inner world at peace even as the external world was violently being shaken. This verse from the prophet Isaiah carries this key of peace: "You will keep in perfect peace all who trust in you, all whose thoughts are fixed on you!" (Isaiah 26:3).

Jesus wants His disciples to overcome the temptation of being overwhelmed by grief. He's saying to them, "Guys, you don't have to succumb to your hearts being troubled by My death." He's telling them to guard their hearts against emotional stress.

Jesus gives them great promises of the more remarkable things to come, and then He repeats His encouragement not to allow their hearts to be troubled: "I am leaving you with a gift—peace of mind and heart. And the peace I give is a gift the world cannot give. So don't be troubled or afraid" (John 14:27).

Jesus calls the disciples to abide in Him and trust Him. He calls them to bear much fruit simply by their connection to Him (see John 15). He encourages them with the work of the Holy Spirit and promises that their sadness will be turned into joy (see John 16).

Jesus continues to talk about the coming persecution. As He's telling the disciples this bad news, they are increasingly impacted by His words. Their hearts are troubled by the conversation. He looks at them and says, "But because I have said these things to you, sorrow has filled your heart" (John 16:6 NKJV).

Sorrow had filled their hearts. Troubling thoughts about what they had heard externally stirred up their internal reality. Things were not going to turn out the way they had thought. Sorrow makes your heart sick. Discouragement and disillusionment stole their hope. "Hope deferred makes the heart sick, but a dream fulfilled is a tree of life" (Proverbs 13:12).

Jesus was preparing the disciples both for His crucifixion and for His resurrection, which would bring fulfillment to their future. They had anchored their hope on Jesus ruling on earth, and on being by His side as He reigned. Their dream was too small.

After His last words in the Upper Room, Jesus walks to the Garden of Gethsemane, and the disciples follow Him. There, He says to them, "Pray that you will not give in to temptation" (Luke 22:40).

Jesus was calling His disciples to fight in the place of prayer so that their hearts would not be overcome by sorrow. In the place of prayer, what's going on in your heart is exposed and seen. Jesus had already given them the answer to their coming temptation in His Upper Room Discourse, telling them these things:

1. Guard your heart, don't let it be troubled; stay connected to Me.
2. Believe in Father God.
3. Believe in Me, Jesus.
4. Receive the coming Holy Spirit.
5. Don't be overcome with sorrow and grief.

The disciples didn't gain the victory amid this challenge, as Jesus did when He prayed so fervently that His sweat fell on the ground as blood. Jesus won the battle in prayer, and an angel strengthened Him. Afterward, "he stood up again and returned to the disciples, only to find them asleep, *exhausted from grief*" (Luke 22:45, emphasis added). The disciples fell asleep not only because they were tired, but because sorrow had taken root in their hearts. Sorrow is the opposite of faith; the sin of unbelief closed their hearts to God.

Only you can steward your heart. Jesus wants to get you free from disappointment and sorrow. He wants to heal your heart and mine, and make us open-hearted again. The hope for your heart comes from the one who lives inside your heart. Jesus is jealous of your whole heart.

How did the disciples find health in their hearts? Jesus prophesied that joy was going to hit their hearts: "So you have sorrow now, but I will see you again; then you will rejoice, and no one can rob you of that joy" (John 16:22). Jesus stayed true to that promise. After His death, the disciples were in the Upper Room again, behind locked doors, fearful that they would be killed just as Jesus had been. Yet even after they had betrayed Him at the cross and had closed up their hearts to Him through sorrow, Jesus broke through their walls and appeared to them:

Suddenly, Jesus was standing there among them! "Peace be with you," he said. As he spoke, he showed them the wounds in his hands and his side. They were *filled with joy when they saw the Lord!* Again he said, "Peace be with you. As the Father has sent me, so I am sending you." Then he breathed on them and said, "Receive the Holy Spirit."

John 20:19–22, emphasis added

The disciples rejoiced because of the joy of Jesus' resurrection. In the Upper Room, Jesus presented Himself as the resurrected Lord. The prescription for sick hearts is gaining a vision of the resurrection.

Healthy Hearts Heal

When our hearts are troubled with discouragement, torment, and sorrow, we open the door to be attacked by the enemy. He attacks during our most vulnerable moments. God uses the sifting of our hearts during seasons of suffering to make us stronger. God does not cause suffering, but He designs a trail of triumph for us to walk through it.

Daily, the primary thing that brings healing in every realm of my life is a healthy heart. Like the disciples, I believe that I can overcome internal struggles more quickly as I focus on the resurrected Jesus. One key verse that anchors my heart is Philippians 3:10 (NASB): "That I may know Him and the power of His resurrection and the fellowship of His sufferings, being conformed to His death."

How do you find heart healing? I focus on gaining a fresh vision of the resurrected Lord by

1. knowing Jesus intimately,
2. positioning my heart before Jesus to heal,
3. fellowshipping with Jesus as I suffer,
4. becoming more like Jesus as I die to self, and
5. envisioning Jesus as my resurrected Lord and healer.

Healing happens daily as you receive a fresh vision of Jesus, the resurrected One, who heals your heart and body. Miraculous encounters with Him bring significant breakthroughs in our lives as we tap into the supernatural power of heaven.

Who's on Your Healing Team?

The Sunday morning after Dre died, we attended UPPERROOM in Dallas, which was meeting at the Christ for the Nations campus. We had taken several weeks off from our Sunday morning responsibilities at the Foursquare Church we were pastoring. I knew I needed to be soaked in Jesus' presence in worship and encounter Him.

I had moved forward as Elyssa Smith led worship. Suddenly, the dance team ran onto the platform. Two strong black men who reminded me of my two Brazilian sons began to dance with flags. The worship team began to sing about the glory around God's throne, and I thought again about my son Dre. Even though Dre had struggled with drugs and alcohol, he loved Jesus. When he was drunk or high, he often told his friends about Jesus.

Zeke's vision of Dre in heaven had comforted my heart. As we continued to sing songs about the glory surrounding God's throne, I had a heavenly picture of Dre. He was in a grassy meadow surrounded by the light and glory of God. His eyes were bright and clear. His big smile reflected heaven's light, and he was being welcomed by my father, Allen. They were laughing together.

At that moment, my heart began the healing process. I entrusted my son to the grace, mercy, and justice of Jesus, the resurrected One.

Whenever someone goes through a crisis, I often ask, "Who's on your healing team?" I mean by that question that God provides people who are safe for us to talk to about the issues we are facing, and who will give us wise counsel and minister the healing of Jesus to our hearts. Also, when you talk about a healing team, it frames the crisis you've just faced with the promise of a positive future.

During the first year after Dre's death, I had several people on my healing team, including Paul Kuzma, a professional counselor provided to pastors of the Foursquare Church. I heard the Lord speak to my heart about also setting up an appointment with Sharla Brenneman, founder of Inner Room ministry and a pastoral leader at UPPERROOM in Dallas.

I enjoyed connecting with Sharla and being able to share some of my history. She talked with me about the importance of healing our hearts. Then she led me through a process of encountering Jesus, who makes our hearts whole. She asked me if I had a vision of Jesus. As we talked, I described a vision that I had seen that week of Jesus as I had been worshiping. As I explained the picture, it became clearer and encouraged my heart. Jesus was dressed as a prince and was kneeling to put beautiful iridescent glass slippers on my feet in the vision. The slippers fit me perfectly, as if they were made to be part of me. We began to dance in a beautiful ballroom part of a castle. There were thrones at the side, covered in red velvet. There was a sparkling carriage outside.

As we were dancing, I saw that I was wearing a beautiful gold crown on my head. The crown was not heavy to wear; it was like a crowning glory or radiance resting upon my head. As we danced, I saw keys hanging decoratively on my flowing gown. I felt completely loved, whole, and connected to Jesus.

It brings a smile to my face as I see the intimate way Jesus appears to each one of us. Whether you are male or female, if Jesus is your Lord, He is also your Bridegroom. Together, we are the Bride of Christ who will celebrate with Him during the wedding feast of the Lamb.

Jesus Heals Hearts and Bodies

When I was ministering to pastors and leaders in Brazil, I saw a vision of Jesus healing hearts. In this vision, I saw the hand of God reaching into chest cavities and massaging hearts. As the hand of God reached into the hearts, I saw the red glow of His presence filling each heart with healing light. I was ministering to a long line of men on that particular night. Some men were instantly touched by God's power and fell in His presence as I laid hands on them. As I prayed and prophesied with a translator, sometimes I would reach out and hug them, and they would instantly fall with the love of God covering them. As God reached in and touched their hearts, He also healed their bodies.

The following day, one of the pastors brought me a white rose with a letter of thanks written in English. Included in his letter was this Scripture: "Praise the LORD! How joyful are those who fear the LORD and delight in obeying his commands. Their children will be successful everywhere; an entire generation of godly people will be blessed" (Psalm 112:1–2).

As I received the pastor's note and rose, I understood why there had been so many men lined up to receive that night. Everyone in the Body of Christ would agree that we need spiritual fathers in our lives to impart spiritual blessing. Over the past generations, however, we have not fully understood how we need spiritual mothers. These spiritual mothers are not required to impart just to the women in the Body of Christ. Men also need the spiritual impartation and blessing that comes through the nurturing force of a mother. Fathers and mothers together reflect the glory of God.

That afternoon, through a translator, I said a word of encouragement to one of the worship pastors who had led us into God's presence the night before. Before the conference, I had prophesied over this young man and his wife. Part of what I said to him after this powerful night of God's presence being poured out was, "I'm proud of you." These simple words made him weep, and he was undone. Later, the translator came to me and said how powerful and confirming my words were. The worship pastor had never heard anyone, not even his earthly father, say, "I'm proud of you."

You may be like this faithful worship pastor. The wounding of your heart may not be from a traumatic event or abuse. Sometimes a deeper wound comes through neglect or abandonment. It's hard to point to something specific that happened to you, yet you sense a void in your heart. Your heart could be hungry for affirmation, so rather than positioning your heart before God for healing, you could fall into the people-pleasing trap. Our churches are filled with people trying to perform well enough to receive an earthly father's blessing. This orphan mentality has made the Church sick. Our hearts need to be healed by the only one who can fill that void—God alone.

In the next chapter, we will look at how you position your heart for healing. First, take a moment, breathe in, and pray this prayer out loud:

Father,
I position myself before You.
I bring my heart to You.
You can see the condition of my heart.
You can see if my heart is divided, bruised, broken, or wounded.

Daddy, you put the lonely in families.
Reach into my heart and fill it with light.
Let the toxins of neglect and abandonment be cleansed.
Reach in and pull out any hidden orphan
mentality or entitlement.
I rest my whole being in Your loving arms.

Jesus, You are the healer of the brokenhearted.
You are kind and compassionate.
Your truth sets us free.

Liberate my heart from lies and false narratives.
Free me from the hidden traumas of the past
and the sorrows of today.

Jesus, I want to see You rightly.
Give me a vision of You as my resurrected Lord.
Create in me a pure heart.
Keep my heart in sync with Your heart.
In Your name, Jesus, Amen.

seven

Surrender

Positioning Your Heart to Be Healed

Michael Miller and his wife, Lorisa, are the founders and lead pastors of a prayer and worship movement called UPPERROOM in Dallas, Texas. In a sermon at UPPERROOM, Michael had this to say about God resurrecting our hurting hearts:

> I believe the Lord wants to give us a new freedom to believe again. He wants us to bring our hearts to Him so He can heal us completely. Heart healing begins with being honest with Jesus.
>
> A liberated heart is the truest act of worship. A heart that has been set free from circumstances and pain is a testimony to the glory of God. We worship Him when we walk by faith in spite of what we've been through. I think it's important for us to believe again with childlike faith.
>
> I experienced a deep disappointment in my life. Things do not always turn out the way you thought they would, especially when you begin to believe God for big things. Sometimes in charismatic

circles, we want to just put a bandage on our pain rather than allowing Jesus to heal our hearts. He wants us to be intimate with Him, and draw from Him as our source.

I was a young adult pastor in a Church of Christ and full of faith for God to do miracles. If you needed healing at our church, you came to me for prayer. I was walking in the purity of revelation that Jesus is our healer. I began to see healing and miracles as I prayed for the sick.

One day I was forwarded a phone call from a desperate parent who said, "My son had a dream last night. In the dream, I called a Church of Christ to ask a pastor to come pray for my son to be healed!"

"What's wrong with your son?" I asked.

"My son Willie is nineteen years old, and he's been sent home with an aggressive form of cancer."

"Yes, I'll be there." I immediately went to their home and developed a relationship with this amazing young man. As we prayed for Willie, God began to move in his life. I was filled with faith that Willie would be healed. I shared the Gospel with the family; we took Communion together and prayed for Willie's healing. Over the coming months, I went to their home over twenty times to pray for healing.

Willie was a freshman at the University of Texas who had to come home halfway through his fall semester. After I prayed with him, he began to radically improve. His tumor began to shrink. By Christmas, his cancer was in remission and he was able to go back to college.

I was so full of faith that God would heal this young man. However, when Willie went back to college in Austin, he had a major relapse with cancer and had to come back home. We continued to pray and believe in God for his complete healing. Even though Willie's numbers go up and down, I'm so full of faith for his healing.

In May of that year, Willie's parent calls me and says, "We got a bad report. Not only has the tumor come back, but it's bigger than before."

We continue to pray for him, and Willie is weaker than I had ever seen him before. In May of 2006, Willie died. His cancer came back so aggressively that it took us all by surprise. Within a two-week period, I went from thinking *Willie is going to be healed* to having to deal with the disappointment of his death.

I'm devastated. This was a vibrant young man. I remember telling the Lord, *God, You have a sick sense of humor. You give a young man a dream about a Church of Christ pastor who prays for his healing, and he's healed. You send me to him to pray for him. God, I did my part, but You didn't do Yours.*

I'm honest with God. I had to go to church that weekend because I was paid to as a pastor. When people stood up and raised their hands to worship God, I sat down with my arms crossed. I was in the back corner of the church, frustrated with the Lord.

I remember the Lord said, *Son, you need to deal with this. You need to deal with this offense. You are offended at Me.*

You're right I'm offended at You, God. I can't deny reality.

I'm just letting the Lord have it. In the back corner of the church, I fell on the ground and said, *Only You can shepherd me through this! I entrust my heart to You.*

That was a Saturday night service. I had a dream that night. Willie's funeral was the next day, on Sunday afternoon. In the dream, I was playing golf, which I love to do. I was playing the Dallas National Golf Club, one of the nicest courses in Texas. The Dallas National has these comfort stations every three holes where you can get anything you want.

I had finished playing my round and was coming off the eighteenth green. Willie comes driving up in a golf cart. During the entire time I knew Willie, he didn't have hair and was very skinny because of chemo. But in this dream Willie had long flowing hair, and he was fit. His arms and legs were muscular.

Willie walks up and gives me this huge hug and says, "That was an amazing round you played at the Dallas National." Then Willie points and says, "Do you see up there in the pro shop? The Head Pro is up there, requesting to talk to you."

I give Willie a hug and walk up to the pro shop. It's so high that it has clouds hitting the windows overlooking the golf course. I walk in and it's glowing with light.

The Head Pro turns and looks at me with piercing eyes and says, "I'm thankful that you played the Dallas National today. But I want to tell you this: Although you played well, that wasn't a normal round at the Dallas National. I want to give you two options." First, he points to this rack of shirts and said, "You can take any of these shirts as a souvenir."

I look at the amazing blue golf shirts that say *Dallas National* on them. I tell the Head Pro, "I love these shirts, but what's my other option?"

He looks at me with intensity, holds up a ticket, and says, "Here's a ticket; you can play the Dallas National again."

In my dream, I didn't hesitate; I grabbed the ticket and said, "I'll be back! I'm going to play another round."

The next day, I remembered the dream as I drove to Willie's funeral in pouring down rain. I was still a bit mad at God and frustrated by the process I'd been through. On the way to the funeral, I tell my wife, Lorisa, about the dream I had, and immediately I begin to get revelation from God about what the dream meant. For me, the Dallas National is "heaven on earth." Our commission is to bring heaven to earth. I had played this round of golf, and Willie drives down with long hair and is healthy and whole—which is heaven's perspective of where Willie now is. Willie tells me the Head Pro wants to talk to me. Who is the Head Pro? Jesus Himself. Jesus, with His piercing eyes, gives my heart two options in light of what I'd been through:

1. I can wear the shirt as a souvenir with the belief that *this is what happens when nineteen-year-olds get cancer—they die.*
2. Or I can take the ticket and *contend again for healing,* knowing that Willie's case wasn't a standard round for heaven coming to earth.

The revelation from this dream liberated my heart. Jesus shepherded my heart through the disappointment and pain of Willie's death. I got a resurrected perspective of Jesus. Although my heart was in pain and I was still grieving, I had a new perspective to see my situation through the lens of the resurrection. It brought healing to my heart and enlarged my capacity to see the mystery of Willie's death from God's perspective. I then had courage to contend again for nineteen-year-olds to be healed of cancer. I've seen at least two teenagers whom I know be healed of cancer since that time.

I believe God is resurrecting our hearts from the dead, disappointed places so we can contend again in faith.[1]

A Healthy, Undivided Heart

All of us have gone through disappointment, pain, and loss. We all need a fresh perspective of the resurrected Lord, who still does miracles today. Having a healthy, undivided heart will bring great joy to our lives.

This Scripture highlights how important it is to have a healed heart: "So above all, guard the affections of your heart, for they affect all that you are. Pay attention to the welfare of your innermost being, for from there flows the wellspring of life" (Proverbs 4:23 TPT).

Those who have given in to fear and unbelief have had their hearts trampled on by the sorrows of life. In these next exercises, we're going to take stock of our hearts. Answer each reflection question with honesty and transparency. Pray this prayer out loud to prepare to hear God's voice:

Jesus, shine Your light on the hidden recesses of my heart.
Show every dark or toxic attitude or thought
so that it can be cleansed by the light of Your presence.
I ready my innermost being to be tested and purified
by the truth of Your Word.

Jesus, I say yes to Your promises.
I will rest in Your faithfulness.
My confidence is in Your goodness.
I anchor my heart on You.
In Your name, Amen.

Healing Moments

FOR YOUR HEART AND HEALTH

- Reflect on your last year(s). Specifically list all the disappointments that you faced. (A disappointment is where your expectations were unmet.)

- Share areas of loss from your last year(s). This could be the loss of a loved one, the loss of a pregnancy, the loss of a job, etc.

- If you have gone through a crisis that's still unresolved, ask the Holy Spirit to show you who's on your healing team. List those potential people on paper (your team could be made up of a small group, a counselor, a pastor, a friend, etc.).

- Ask the Holy Spirit to show you areas where you have allowed unbelief to invade your heart. These can sometimes be places of delayed promises, like a sickness that has yet to be totally healed or a relationship that needs mending. Specifically list these areas.

- How have you dealt with these areas of disappointment, loss, and unbelief? Have you talked more about them with Jesus or with other people? Have you looked for your comfort from people or from God? (Be honest. I've found that while it's important for me to have safe people whom I can process life with and who can pray for me, deep healing comes from encountering Jesus Himself.)

- In the midst of the painful things of your last year(s), what promises has Jesus whispered into your heart? Write down the promises and Scriptures He has given you.

- Do you have spiritual fathers or mothers in your life? If not, take a moment and ask Holy Spirit to reveal who those people could be. If you do have someone who pours into you like a mother or father, take a moment this week to send that person a thank-you card.

- Is your heart in sync with the words of Jesus? Are you able to be in His presence and have joy and peace fill your heart? If so, write a prayer of thanksgiving. If not, write a prayer of desperation and need. (If you feel depressed or in turmoil, schedule an appointment with your pastor, your counselor, or someone who ministers as a heart healer.)

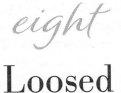
eight

Loosed

Set Free from a Spirit of Infirmity

Author and speaker Leslie Tracey carries the mantle of the prophetic with 4 Corners Alliance and travels with Joan Hunter. After a healing miracle in her life, Leslie also became a co-founder of Double Portion Ministries, with her friend Barbara Rucci. Leslie recounted her healing story in a *Healing Rain* podcast interview:

> I was blessed with a believing mom who brought us to church. My husband and I raised our children to love God and serve Him in church. One morning we started our day normally, getting the kids to school and going to work. But our day did not end typically. Our day ended in a hospital emergency room after my husband had a heart attack. It was sudden, with no warning signs; my husband was young and healthy.
>
> When I saw the surgical team come down the hallway, I thought, *This can't be good.* They had dire expressions on their faces.

The news was not good. "We do not expect your husband to live through the night," the head of the surgical team said. "If he does live through the night, he will be completely paralyzed."

The doctor discovered that a blood clot had lodged in my husband's brain. He was resting in a semi-coma and was already paralyzed. This catastrophe spun our family into a crisis.

My husband exceeded expectations, lived through the night, and has now, years later, recovered his ability to walk. But at the time, I was not at all prepared for this level of health crisis. I had been raised in a grounded, born-again home filled with the Word, but it had never rooted in my heart. I had a lot of head knowledge, but I wasn't living a powerful, victorious life. The trauma of the evening overwhelmed me. I felt a gut punch to my stomach and immediately began to get sick. Instantly, a digestive disorder began that had me doubled over in pain. My husband slowly recovered and was sent to a rehab hospital, but doctors sent me to a different hospital.

I later underwent surgery to take out most of my intestine. This surgery was supposed to solve all the pain I was experiencing and stop the destruction from what was going on internally. Surgery did not stop the symptoms, however, nor the progression of the disease. I spent a lot of my days medicated, in bed. I could relate to the story of the woman with the issue of blood and how she spent all she had on the physicians, which only made her condition worse.

I was sent from one doctor to another. Nobody seemed to have the answer. I know now that this was because it was a spiritual issue. Some days I would feel well enough to go to church, and I would get prayer at the end of the service. I would have other Bible-believing people pray for me. Some symptoms would go temporarily, but they always came back.

I began to change my beliefs on healing. *Maybe God just doesn't want to heal me*, I thought. I changed what I believed based on my circumstances. We lost finances. My husband wasn't working; he was then in a wheelchair. I wasn't working because I was homebound. Much of the time, I was in bed, depressed.

I was losing most of my relationships because many people don't want to be around someone who is constantly sick. My children couldn't comprehend the narrative of what had just happened to both of their parents. We did not have a happy home.

I had one friend, Barbara Rucci, who stuck through this with me. One day she called me, and I was bundled up in bed. I was darkly depressed that day, counseling myself out of my soul.

"There's a healing evangelist coming to our city," Barbara said to me. "On Sunday morning, she's going to have a healing service. I think we should go."

"Absolutely not," I said. "I'm not going. I have been prayed for at least five hundred times. I've given up on ever being healed. I have no faith for this anymore."

I was so wrapped in self-pity. I was so mad at Barbara. *She doesn't know what I'm going through*, I thought. *She doesn't know what it would take to go to church. She has a great life. She's healthy, has a great family, and has plenty of money. She doesn't know what it takes for me to attend church.*

To go to church I would have to medicate myself, and that would mean falling asleep. If I didn't take medication, it would be so painful. I wouldn't be able to sit through a service. Even the most comfortable chairs in the church were excruciatingly painful for me. With my digestive disorder, I wasn't getting the nutrition I needed, either. I just didn't have the energy to sit there.

Nobody knows the pain and struggle I go through! I thought. I was so angry that Barbara had even suggested that I go. I felt alone and misunderstood. But my friend would not let up.

"I believe God is saying that we need to go to this healing service," Barbara said. "This is what's going to happen. I'll come over to your house and sit in your driveway, honking my horn, until you come out. It's going to be early Sunday morning, so your neighbors won't enjoy that."

Sunday came. I got up and stumbled around trying to get ready. I went to church angry, with a bad attitude. Eva Dooley and her husband, Bill, have spent forty years traveling nationally and internationally as healing evangelists.[1] Eva had traveled to my city of Chicago from Texas for this healing service. When Eva walked into the room, she had the piercing eyes of the Lord.

"Someone here has suffered for so long and so intensely with an intestinal issue, and God is going to heal you today," Eva said right away.

She got into the pulpit and preached the Word, and God showed up. At the end of the message, she asked, "Where's the person who has suffered so long and intensely with an intestinal issue? Come forward for healing."

I had no faith that I could be healed. I didn't even go forward. She had ten people respond, but I sat there. *If God wants to heal me, He can heal me in my seat*, I thought. I was making up my own rules. At this point, because of the chronic sickness, I was disobedient and rebellious in my heart.

"Get up there and get your healing right now," Barbara said. She took her elbow and rammed it into me.

I wanted to argue with Barbara. We were sitting in the front of the church; I didn't want to make a scene. Rather than being disruptive, I went up front and joined the line of people. People were getting healed as Eva prayed.

I was saying to God, *Lord, I can't go through one more time of being prayed for and having all the symptoms come back. I don't have it in me. I would rather be sick for the rest of my life than get my hopes up and be disappointed.*

"I think I might be the person you were talking about," I whispered to Eva when she got to me. I could feel the battle in the spirit realm as Eva looked at me with her intense eyes.

"You are the person," Eva replied. "God told me He is going to heal you. A spirit of trauma has attached itself to you physically, emotionally, mentally, and financially. A spirit of trauma has stolen relationships from you."

As she spoke, I could see the faces of friends who were no longer in my life. I'm not blaming anyone; I couldn't have held on that long in the relationship. Even my children couldn't understand when I couldn't make their baseball games or sporting events. I couldn't go because I was sick at home. This spirit of trauma had taken so much from our family.

"I'm loosing you from the spirit of trauma, and you're going to get healed," Eva said. "I loose you in the name of Jesus from a spirit of trauma."

She didn't pray a long, extensive prayer; she loosed me in the name above all other words, *Jesus*. I felt a boom in the spirit, almost like a dynamite stick exploded inside me. I woke up on the floor. From the floor, I could hear Eva speaking over me: "God will use you to bring thousands upon thousands of people out of darkness through your testimony," she prophesied.

I have never seen another hospital bed again. I have never seen the endless cycle of going in and out of the hospital or in and out of the doctor's office. It was broken that day! I was so thankful that Eva named what was going on in my life. It was a demonic spirit.

About a week and a half later, some symptoms began to come back, but this time I knew what it was. I knew it was a spirit of trauma. So I used the Word of God, and I commanded the spirit of trauma to stop harassing me with symptoms. I was not going to go back to that sick bed any longer! I was not going to come into agreement with the symptoms!

Leslie smiled as she finished sharing this powerful testimony of healing and deliverance.[2]

Don't Agree with Sickness

When a health condition in our lives moves from temporary to chronic, we are tempted to allow our hearts to be troubled. Now, it's no longer just what's happening to your physical body; it's what is going on inside your heart:

- Your thoughts carry on an internal dialogue and narrative.
- Your emotions are riddled with self-pity.

- Your self-pity isolates you from relationships.
- Your identity gets wrapped around being a victim of sickness.
- Your troubled heart opens the door to the demonic.

If the devil can deceive you, he can make you think you are powerless against his attacks. Don't allow yourself to come into agreement with sickness. I live in the United States, where health care is available. Most people I know go to the doctor for their symptoms before they ever spend any time praying about them. The devil doesn't play fair. He roams around like a lion seeking to devour you and your family. This Bible passage provides practical instructions on resisting the enemy:

> Be self-controlled and vigilant always, for your enemy the devil is always about, prowling like a lion roaring for its prey. Resist him, standing firm in your faith and remember that the strain is the same for all your fellow-Christians in other parts of the world. And after you have borne these sufferings a very little while, God himself (from whom we receive all grace and who has called you to share his eternal splendor through Christ) will make you whole and secure and strong. All power is his for ever and ever, amen!
>
> 1 Peter 5:8–11 PHILLIPS

Let's look more closely at these instructions or practical steps from Peter on how to resist the enemy:

1. *Be self-controlled and vigilant.* A lack of self-control opens the door to sin, sickness, and the demonic realm. Allow the Holy Spirit to show you healthy guidelines for your life. Cut things out of your life that open the door to compromise.
2. *Don't allow yourself to be isolated.* The enemy is a predator who tries to cut you off from relationships and

community. Father God puts the lonely in families. It's essential for you to find a safe place where you can do life with other believers.

3. *Resist the devil.* Guard your heart against the enemy (see Proverbs 4:23). Resist the devil's narrative in your mind. Watch out for things like self-pity or unforgiveness in your heart. Your internal resistance of the enemy is as important as the external words you speak.

4. *Stand firm on the Word.* Continue to resist the enemy by speaking the words of Scripture. Know your authority to bind and loose the enemy (see Matthew 16:19; 28:18). Abide with Jesus and pray without ceasing (see John 15; 1 Thessalonians 5:16–18). Demons cannot read your mind; they are not all-knowing, as God is. Speak out loud when you are confronting demons.

5. *Fellowship with Jesus and others when you suffer.* Jesus does not cause sickness or suffering, but He allows it and uses it in our lives to make us more like Him. It's a sifting process. Allow the suffering to help you die to selfish or self-centered thinking or ambitions of your heart. Become more like Jesus in the suffering (see Philippians 3:10), but also expect God to give you a fresh revelation of your resurrected Lord to receive resurrection power.

6. *Receive wholeness for your heart and health.* As you allow Jesus to sift out negative attitudes and purify your heart, receive His wholeness. His inheritance for you is a whole heart—not a divided heart, not a wounded heart, not a broken heart. As He heals your heart, He also restores your health. Don't allow any narratives in your mind to embrace a defeated lifestyle. Contend for complete healing in areas of physical need.[3]

7. *Become mature and secure in God.* A mark of maturity is joy. Joy is your strength. If you are not walking in joy, it

is a marker that you need more of Jesus and need to grow more mature in Him. Anchor your security on Him while you wait on God for your prayers to be answered and His promises to be fulfilled.

8. *Stand strong as you pray for others.* As you resist the enemy internally by guarding your heart, and externally by speaking the Word, you will gain strength. Rather than walking with human strength or bravado, walk boldly, clothed in God's power. God's kind of strength is found when you go to Him in weakness. As you are anointed with His power and zeal, you will be amazed at how bold you become as you pray on behalf of others.

The Problem of Unbelief

One of the things that happened to Leslie when she was so sick was that she stopped believing it was God's will to heal her. She began to anchor what she felt on her experience rather than on what the Bible says.

Some who call themselves Christians have a worldview in which they don't believe in angels, demons, heaven, or hell. The overall view of demonization from my professors at Vanderbilt University Divinity School was that demonic spirits don't exist. They would refer to the "demon of drink" as a result of someone's poor choices.

I am thankful for the full scholarship I received to attend Vanderbilt. It was God's provision while my husband and I were planting and pastoring our first church as I attended seminary. Sometimes, the lessons we learn in such an atmosphere can help us better understand the world. However, unbelief entered my heart through the liberal teaching. When our house caught on fire two months after I graduated, we were thrown into crisis mode.

After talking to our pastoral supervisor, he invited us to attend an inner healing and deliverance training conference for pastors and leaders. We had to battle to get to this event. As I mentioned in the introduction, I was delivered at that conference from demons of religion and rejection. I came away so free from the inside out that I wanted everyone to be free.[4]

A wonderful thing about being delivered from demonic oppression is that the stronghold of the demonic narrative, which has been troubling your heart through thoughts and emotions, is ripped out. There's such a newfound freedom from the inside out that other people can see the freedom in your eyes and countenance.

After I was delivered, the Word of God came alive to me. The Word became my standard and my plumb line.

Demons and Sickness

Do demons ever cause sickness in the Bible? Scripture contains numerous examples of sickness being connected with demonic oppression. One example is found in Mark 9:20–22:

> So they brought the boy. But when the evil spirit saw Jesus, it threw the child into a violent convulsion, and he fell to the ground, writhing and foaming at the mouth.
> "How long has this been happening?" Jesus asked the boy's father.
> He replied, "Since he was a little boy. The spirit often throws him into the fire or into the water, trying to kill him. Have mercy on us and help us, if you can."

When I was in seminary, my New Testament professor pointed out that this was a primitive society that called sicknesses like this demons when people didn't understand that it was epilepsy.

However, the book of Mathew distinguishes between epilepsy and demonic activity in those whom Jesus healed:

> News about him spread as far as Syria, and people soon began bringing to him all who were sick. And whatever their sickness or disease, or if they were *demon-possessed or epileptic* or paralyzed—he healed them all.
>
> Matthew 4:24, emphasis added

The boy with the symptoms of epilepsy in Mark 9:22 had a demonic spirit that was throwing him into the fire. When a demonic spirit is attached to trauma in our lives, the physical symptoms often go beyond what's normal for a particular ailment. You can see from Matthew 4:24 that the Bible distinguishes between a physical condition of epilepsy and demonic oppression.

Be Available to Pray

When I minister healing, I minister to the whole person. I ask the Holy Spirit to show me the root issue. John Wimber greatly impacted me with his teaching on the Kingdom of God.[5] He encouraged every believer to regularly pray for others and expect to see signs, wonders, and miracles as they prayed. One of the reasons I appreciate John Wimber's approach is that it empowers every believer to put into practice the gifts of the Holy Spirit.

As a young pastor, I began to experience supernatural healings by just being available to God at any moment of the day to pray for people. I was playing in a tennis match one day at a local sports facility when one of the women on the opposing team fell with a scream. I had shaken hands with the woman for the first time before we began to play, so I didn't know what she believed. However, most of the time when people are in pain, they are open to our prayers.

I got down on my knees and asked her how she was doing. She said, "I heard a loud pop; I'm afraid to move my ankle."

"Can I pray for you?" I asked.

She nodded with tears in her eyes. Her language had clued me in to one thing she was dealing with—fear. So I just started by praying the Word of God: *Lord, I thank You that You have not given us a spirit of fear, but of power, love, and a sound mind, as the Bible says in 2 Timothy 1:7. In Your name, Jesus, I rebuke every spirit of fear, and I command it to be under my new friend's feet.*

I began to feel heat flowing through my hands into her ankle, and I went on: *Lord, I release Your healing right now. Father, I pray that every ligament, cartilage, and muscle line up perfectly. I pray that she would have no long-term impact from this injury. Thank You for healing her right now. In Jesus' name, Amen.*

I encouraged her to get up and try to do what she couldn't do only a moment before. As she got up, she was amazed. She could walk on her ankle and was completely fine. We stood around for the rest of the match talking about Jesus.

Now, the critic will say that maybe she wasn't injured in the first place. However, she was in pain enough to be lying on the ground and screaming, wondering if an ambulance needed to be called. I believe that by rebuking the spirit of fear, it was possible to release God's healing immediately.

I used this example because sometimes we need to be available to pray, and God will answer immediately if we are open.

God wants to use every Christian to heal, not just super giants of faith or healing evangelists.

Hindrances to Healing

What are the hindrances to healing? I appreciate the vulnerability of Leslie Tracey's testimony. She does a good job of identifying the false beliefs in her mind. Let me highlight a few hindrances from her testimony:

1. *Unresolved trauma*—All trauma needs healing. God didn't make us to live in continuous trauma.

2. *Having head knowledge about healing, but not believing from the heart*—It's in tough times that you can find out what you truly believe. The center of our belief system is what we believe to be true in our hearts.

3. *Relying on only medical professionals to heal you*—We should be grateful for medical professionals, but we need to seek Jesus, our Great Physician, first, and then proceed with getting medical help. When I struggled with chronic pain from my knees, I inquired of the Lord, whose word to me was *The miracle is in the surgery*. I had a double knee replacement, healed supernaturally, and have had no pain.

4. *Unbelief, believing it isn't God's will to heal*—Unbelief comes in many forms, but it always stands opposed to the will of God. The sin of unbelief includes choosing to agree with the enemy's will for your life rather than God's will for your life.

5. *Isolation from the community of faith*—The enemy seeks to isolate you, to be able to keep you from receiving your healing.

6. *Self-pity*—With self-pity, you have an ongoing dialogue with your pain. This internal narrative blocks you from receiving God's best.

7. *Identity wrapped around sickness*—Rather than knowing you are loved, chosen, empowered, and delighted in as God's son or daughter, you begin to identify yourself according to your disease. You find yourself telling the story of your condition. Your life is wrapped around the limitations of the sickness.

8. *A rebellious, stubborn heart, and offense toward God*—Leslie got to the point where she didn't even want to go forward

for prayer. She felt that if God "wanted to heal her," He could do it where she was sitting.

9. *A troubled heart that opens the door to demonic oppression*— In Leslie's case, the spirit of trauma entered immediately after her husband's heart attack. However, for some people, the demonic oppression gains a foothold when the sickness becomes chronic, lasting an extended period.

All these areas of the heart hinder God's healing in your life. Healing your heart opens the pathway for your body to be healed. Or, as in Leslie's case, the casting out of the spirit of trauma led to healing her body, which led to healing her heart. God wants to heal the whole person.

Be Compassionate

The list above is for self-diagnosis of your own heart and whether anything in it can hinder God's healing in your body. This list is not intended to help you be judgmental of your friends. In the next chapter, we will dig deep and apply this teaching to our own lives. As we close, pray this prayer out loud.

God, You are my healer.
Shine Your light on every hidden and
unresolved trauma in my life.
I know that You didn't create me to live in torment.
You made me to live in health and to prosper.

Jesus, You are my compassionate Lord.
Help me fellowship with You when I am suffering.
Help me become more like You.
I choose to die to the things that keep me from
intimate connection with You.

You are my resurrected Lord;
help me embrace Your resurrection power in my life.

Holy Spirit, You are my Advocate.
I choose to forgive people who don't
understand what I'm going through.
Thank You that You are always
guiding me toward the truth.
Help my heart comprehend and hold on to
the truth of who Jesus is.
Rinse me of unbelief, isolation, and self-pity.
Reveal to me afresh my identity of who I am in Christ.

Jesus, everlasting Lord,
I repent of every rebellious thought and internal dialogue.
I position my heart to be wholly healed by Your love.
I bring before You the areas in my body
that need Your healing.
[List all the areas in which you are believing for healing.]
In faith, I receive Your peace.
I believe that You are good.
I believe that You care for me.
Jesus, I believe You are the same
yesterday, today, and forever.
I receive Your healing in faith.
I love You. In Your name, Amen.

nine

Freed

Deliverance out of Darkness, into Light

Jesus, if You're real, get me out of this, Sean prayed.

Today, Sean Smith Sr. is an author, a prophet, and the founder of R.O.A.R., which stands for Rise of a Remnant.[1] But that night, as second-in-command of a gang, Sean didn't know if he would live or die. Sean knew that if God didn't do a miracle on his behalf, he would be killed for trying to leave the gang. Standing strong as a man who had earned his leadership position the hard way, Sean didn't move. The gang leader kept looking at him, trying to figure out what had changed.

It was no problem with the gang leader that Sean played drums at a local church. Sean had an agreement with a few church elders that he would supply them with marijuana, and they would pay him to play drums. But on this particular Tuesday night, everything changed. Sean was radically saved, was filled with the Holy Spirit, and spoke in tongues:

Now Sean was at this prearranged meeting with the entire gang. As second-in-command, he stood next to the gang leader. As he stood there, he was trusting God for a miracle.

"I don't know what's happened, but you don't belong here anymore," the gang leader said. From that moment, Sean was excommunicated from the gang. Usually, the only way out of the gang was to die or be killed.

That was a miraculous night for Sean. His life had been tough for him as a kid, after his mom's death when he was eleven. Sean stopped talking for almost a year, and his father had him placed in a mental institution for six months. When he was released, his father dropped him off at an adoption home for the next six months. During that year of being away from his dad, a root of bitterness and anger grew in Sean.

Things went sharply downhill for Sean as he got into more and more substance abuse. By the age of fourteen, he was an alcoholic. While most people go through a process to get off drugs and alcohol, Sean experienced immediate deliverance on the night he was saved. From the moment of his salvation, he no longer had a taste for alcohol. He also had no more desire for nicotine or marijuana. Immediately when he was filled with the Holy Spirit, he was free from drugs and alcohol. Sean continues his story:

Getting off alcohol and drugs wasn't the tough part for me. Forgiving my dad was the primary struggle in my faith. It took me a decade to wrestle with my anger and bitterness toward Dad and finally decide to forgive him.

My dad struggled with taking ownership of his responsibility in our relationship. He continued to see me as the problem and couldn't see his abandonment of me when Mom died.

I had already been serving as youth pastor for years, and now I was on my way to being ordained and installed as a senior pastor. Four carloads of my friends were driving four hours to the ordination service. In the middle of our drive, God dealt with my heart. I heard the Lord say, *If you don't forgive him, I'll shut your ministry down.*

What? I asked God.

Call your father right now and forgive him. I'll shut it all down if you don't do it, God told me sternly.

I called my dad and said, "Hey, Dad, I don't want to talk about anything; I just need to tell you something. I'm on my way to be installed as a senior pastor. We're getting ready to launch a new church. When I get home, I want to show you my certification. I want to show it to you."

"Sean, I'm proud of you."

His dad's words shocked Sean. He had never heard his dad say anything positive like that before. Sean began to weep so hard that he had to pull the car over and allow someone else to drive. It was exactly what he needed at that moment. He was able to, at last, forgive his dad from the heart.

In fact, everyone in the car was impacted by the reconciliation of father and son and began to weep. The Holy Spirit showed up powerfully. Out of obedience, Sean had followed the Lord's call to forgiveness and his life was forever changed. His relationship with his dad was forever healed. He concludes,

I needed to get out of my flesh, and out of my emotions, and choose to forgive. I was an emotional wreck when it came to my dad. But now, everything shifted. From that point until my dad's death years later, Dad was with me all the time. He became my best friend and biggest supporter.

Experiencing the Miracle of Redemption

The heavenly Father loved Sean so much that He gave His Son Jesus to die on the cross for Sean's sins. When Sean activated his faith, believed in Jesus, and received Him as his Lord and Savior,

God began the miracle of redemption in Sean's life. To understand the power of this miracle, let's break it down.

1. *Justification* occurs when Jesus frees us from the penalty of sin. We are given a right relationship with God based on the righteousness of Jesus. You and I don't earn this relationship; it's a gift we receive. The cost of sin is eternally eliminated from our lives. In justification, we accept Jesus as our Messiah.

2. *Sanctification* is our lifelong journey as Christians. Even though we were justified through salvation, Jesus continues to free us from the power of sin in our everyday lives. He continues to sanctify us until our life in this world is complete. In sanctification, we receive Jesus as our High Priest.

3. *Glorification* is the fulfillment of our salvation, when we no longer live in this world but live eternally with Jesus. We receive a glorified body in His presence. In glorification, we receive Jesus as our Bridegroom.

Redemption is the whole process of justification, sanctification, and glorification. In your spiritual journey, you experience Jesus as your Messiah, High Priest, and Bridegroom.

On a Tuesday evening, Sean's justification came suddenly when he saw his need for a Savior and repented of his sins. He remembers being filled with the Holy Spirit and speaking in tongues while lying under the third pew in the church building. He asked God to do a miracle and deliver him from the gang lifestyle.

Sean was able to quit drugs and alcohol right away. His sanctification process brought more profound healing in his heart over time, through the power of forgiveness. When he finally forgave his dad after ten years of struggle, he experienced not only reconciliation with his earthly father, but a blessing from his heavenly Father.

The Religious Unsaved

Have you been part of the religious unsaved? Sean's salvation journey did not begin when he started attending church. In fact, after drumming during worship, he remembers going to the green room and smoking joints with a couple of the deacons. He was being paid as a drummer in the church, and he was the drug dealer to the deacons!

Lord, have mercy on the state of the Church. When I hear stories like this about the local Church, I find myself interceding with this conditional promise from Scripture: "If My people who are called by My name will humble themselves, and pray and seek My face, and turn from their wicked ways, then I will hear from heaven, and will forgive their sin and heal their land" (2 Chronicles 7:14 NKJV). What are the conditions of this promise? Here they are:

If we, God's people, the Church, will

1. humble ourselves,
2. pray and seek God's face, and
3. turn from our wicked ways,

then God will

1. hear from heaven,
2. forgive our sin, and
3. heal our land.

This is a corporate call for the global Church. When Wayne and I were planting and pastoring our first church, I had an open vision that awakened my heart to pray for the religious unsaved in our community. In my vision, I saw skeletons sitting at a dining room table. I saw skeletons driving cars up the hill in our neighborhood. I then saw skeletons sitting in the pews at church, singing hymns, and saying prayers. Next to the skeletons, I saw flashes of vibrant color that were the people who were truly saved by Jesus and living a redeemed life. I began to see how religion blinded many people to the power of Jesus in their lives.

Jared and Hannah Scott recently spent three months as missionaries in Spain serving as worship leaders in a local congregation. But Jared Scott was once an unbelieving church attendee. He attended the Southwestern Assemblies of God University and spent a decade in the church, going to college and leading worship, before he truly encountered Jesus as his Savior. Jared describes his transition from being one of the religious unsaved to becoming truly saved:

> I was deeply religious. For ten years before I met the Lord, I was constantly striving to please Him. Working myself to exhaustion, I thought, *Maybe the next thing I do will be enough, so I can measure up to what Jesus paid for*. I had an orphan mindset.
>
> The atmosphere of my early life was one of much brokenness. Though my parents were present when I was young, they were both profoundly dependent on drugs. Ultimately, this led to my siblings and me moving in with my great-grandparents by the time I was four.
>
> But even in that home, I experienced abuse from other relatives. The trauma I had from abandonment and abuse played into the false narrative of my mind that I would never be enough. I was convinced that *everyone is going to leave, and it's my fault*.
>
> In the back of my mind, I never thought I would be good enough. When I met the Father for the first time, I realized I wasn't lacking anything; He already loved me—good, bad, and ugly. That experience of His love totally healed me of this insecurity that had plagued me. I've been aware of His presence with me ever since I met Him.

Salvation Is a Miracle

All of us who come to Jesus at the foot of the cross bring our brokenness to Him to be healed. Attending church is not enough for most people to become free of brokenness and addiction. Attending church can be like a vaccination against the real power of salvation.

Are you a prodigal who needs to come home?

In a season of rebellion, a friend of mine married an alcoholic who didn't know Jesus. She then constantly suffered the sorrow and trauma of being married to an addict. One night after her husband had passed out on the couch after drinking, she turned on the television. Billy Graham was preaching, and her heart was convicted of her own rebellion. This friend had truly known the love of Jesus as a child and teenager. She was a prodigal who needed to come home. She knelt down and surrendered her life to Jesus. Her prodigal heart was healed.

My friend's recommitment to Jesus gave her the courage to remove herself and her children from the ongoing trauma of her husband's alcohol abuse. As a single mother with a houseful of children, she had to work full-time to meet the demands of her bills. God miraculously provided for her again and again. Her house was filled with peace because of Jesus. After several years of being a single mom, God gave her a loving and tender husband and restored her household. God is a redeemer.

Do You Need More of Jesus?

Let's learn from these stories we looked at of people God has saved, healed, and delivered:

- Leslie Tracey was delivered from a spirit of trauma that opened the door to constant sickness.

- Sean Smith Sr. was saved, immediately delivered from drug addiction, and supernaturally spared from being murdered when he left a gang. His heart was healed when he forgave his father.
- Jared Scott was religious but unsaved. He was delivered from constantly striving to please God when he truly met Jesus and realized he was already loved by the Father.
- My friend was saved young, but in a time of rebellion married an unsaved alcoholic. She surrendered her heart and came home as a prodigal. God redeemed her home with peace, provision, and a godly husband.

In simple terms, *we all need more of Jesus*.

Deliverance is helping people come out of darkness and into His marvelous light. It makes me think of this promise:

> But you are a chosen generation, a royal priesthood, a holy nation, His own special people, that you may proclaim the praises of Him who called you out of darkness into His marvelous light; who once were not a people but are now the people of God, who had not obtained mercy but now have obtained mercy.
>
> 1 Peter 2:9–10 NKJV

When Lazarus was raised from the dead by Jesus, he still needed someone to come alongside him and help loose him from the graveclothes (see John 11:38–44). Deliverance is rescuing someone from bondage.

Because of what Jesus did on the cross, believers already have eternal victory over Satan and demons. However, there can be areas of woundedness or unconfessed sin that allow open doors to the enemy to attack a person. Part of the journey through this book is closing any doors to the enemy that might be open without your being aware of it. The following questions will help you become aware of those doors you need to close.

Healing Moments
FOR YOUR HEART AND HEALTH

1. Take a moment to reflect on the joy of your salvation. After reading this chapter, do you believe God is calling you to make a fresh commitment to Him? Are you a prodigal who is coming home to Jesus and the family of God? Is there someone in your life whom you are praying for to receive Jesus as his or her Savior and Lord?

2. Are you completely surrendered to Jesus? Ask the Holy Spirit to search your mind right now and show you if there is anything you are doing or participating in that does not bring God pleasure. Write down whatever He says.

3. Have you forgiven everyone who has hurt you from your heart? Take out a blank sheet of paper and ask the Holy Spirit to bring to mind any people you've not entirely forgiven. After listing their names, spend time forgiving each person. (If you need an outline of how to forgive from the heart, download the free resource from my website that I mentioned earlier: *5 Steps of Grace: A Journey Guide to Freedom*.[2])

4. Remember and write about how you first came to Christ. What problems were you facing? How did you know that you needed a Savior? Were there people God used to lead you to Himself? How did your life change after you received Christ? What is your life

like now? Write out your testimony, and then write down one person you know who doesn't know Christ. Begin to ask God for an opportunity to share your testimony with that person.

ten

Faith

Moving Mountains through Prayer

Pastor Silas and Pastora Carmen Zdrojewski lead a ten-thousand-member church in Curitiba, Brazil, called *Primeira Igreja do Evangelho Quadrangular*. I was preaching at their church recently, when Carmen told me this story:

> I was pregnant with my second baby; everything was going well until I started to drop things. I was losing strength in my hands. Whether things were light or heavy, I would lose my grip, and they would slip out of my hands.
>
> I was diagnosed with Raynaud's syndrome in the fifth month of my pregnancy, a rare disorder that causes the blood vessels in fingers or toes to constrict or have spasms. The doctor was concerned that I couldn't carry my baby full term. He injected me with corticosteroids to help the baby's lungs mature before being born.
>
> At the beginning of the eighth month of pregnancy, I knew something was wrong. I didn't feel well, so I called the doctor,

and he had me come in immediately. My blood pressure was dangerously high. I was very swollen, and even my toes began to bleed because of the swelling. The doctor put me in the hospital because preeclampsia was dangerous for the baby and me.

I went into the hospital on Friday night, and by Saturday, my blood pressure was continuing to rise. The doctor asked to see my husband, Silas.

"I don't know if your wife is going to survive," the doctor told him. "I also don't know if your baby will live. I needed to tell you so that you could prepare yourself."

Pastor Silas is a man of prayer. His family has faithfully served *Primeira Igreja do Evangelho Quadrangular* in Curitiba for many years. He continued telling me the story:

As I began to pray, God gave me a vision. I saw a very dark cloud over the whole hospital. I knew we were in a huge spiritual battle. I called my father, who was the senior pastor at that time.

My father, Pastor Eduardo, was a mighty man of prayer. He called the whole church to fast and pray for my wife, Carmen, and baby Vanessa. At 9:00 a.m. Sunday, the entire church was battling in prayer. At that same time on Sunday morning, baby Vanessa was born. They had been worried about her ability to survive and thought baby Vanessa would need to be transferred to neonatal ICU. God was so good; Vanessa's lungs were fine after her birth. The whole church rejoiced that Vanessa was healthy and didn't need to go to ICU.

The church continued to fast and pray for Carmen and Vanessa. Because it was a life-threatening situation, people were scheduled to pray every fifteen minutes around the clock.

We battled for Carmen's life. The doctor had hoped that Carmen's kidneys would improve and her blood pressure would go down after the C-section. Carmen was still fighting for her life. She couldn't sit up or get out of bed because she was too dizzy. They kept baby Vanessa in an incubator. Carmen's kidneys appeared to be shutting down. The church continued fasting and praying for Carmen's life on Monday, Tuesday, Wednesday, and Thursday.

On Thursday, my father, Pastor Eduardo, went to the hospital in the late afternoon to lay hands on Carmen and pray for her life. When he was praying, he saw a vision. He saw two long-sleeved hands reaching out to Carmen. In these hands from heaven were two brand-new kidneys. After this vision and my father's prayer, Carmen began to recover.

The doctor did a new examination on Carmen and was so surprised. "I see new kidneys!" the doctor exclaimed. "I don't understand; you have new kidneys!"

Carmen finished telling the rest of this amazing story:

I give all the glory and the honor to Jesus that I no longer have damage to my kidneys. I have new kidneys.

God worked a miracle through the church's intercession, prayer, and fasting, and Jesus miraculously healed me. The doctor said I would have to be on blood pressure medication for the rest of my life and that I might have kidney problems. I left the hospital with a box of this blood pressure medication, and it was only this box that I took, and then never again. The Lord brought me healing and gave me back my life and my daughter's life—something that the earthly doctor couldn't guarantee.

I had the Doctor of doctors, the Great Physician, Jesus. It was Jesus who performed this great miracle! I give Him all the glory and honor and the praise.

Authority and Power to Perform Miracles

I was riding in the car in Brazil with Pastor Silas, Pastora Carmen, Vanessa, and Soorin Backer when they told me this miraculous story. Vanessa is now 31 years of age, married, with one healthy son, and in ministry at the church. As they related this miracle, I reflected on how much authority and power the Church has been given. Jesus said in Matthew 28:18–20,

I have been given all authority in heaven and on earth. Therefore, go and make disciples of all the nations, baptizing them in the name of the Father and the Son and the Holy Spirit. Teach these new disciples to obey all the commands I have given you. And be sure of this: I am with you always, even to the end of the age.

The word for *authority* in verse 18 is *exousia*, which means "delegated authority, ability, privilege capacity." Jesus demonstrated His authority to forgive sin, heal sickness, and cast out demons. During this Great Commission, Jesus gave His authority to us as disciples to preach, teach, heal, and deliver.

The Church in Brazil has carried the fires of revival for many years. When I think about this miracle of Carmen's healing, there are some important things this church models for us that we need to be as the Church today:

1. *A praying church:* This church moved into action, and people were scheduled to pray every fifteen minutes around the clock to defeat the enemy through prayer. They understood that it was a life-or-death battle. As a practice, the men of the church pray this way from 8:00 p.m. to 8:00 a.m. every day of the week. During the day, different ministries and departments take two-hour shifts so that they are covered in prayer as a church 24/7.

2. *A fasting church:* This church knew that fasting is a powerful weapon against the enemy. They moved into action and called the entire church to fast.

3. *A believing church:* The people respected the work of the earthly doctor, but believed that they had a Great Physician named Jesus who heals today. They activated their faith and moved into action in unity.

4. *A supernatural church:* God guided them and gave them visions as they prayed. Pastor Silas had a vision of a dark cloud covering the entire hospital, and he knew they were

fighting a spiritual battle. Pastor Eduardo laid hands on Carmen and saw the two kidneys being held in outstretched hands from heaven. This vision preceded the doctor's exclamation, "You have new kidneys!"

We have been given great authority and power from heaven. We need to activate our faith and rise up as a Church in unity. In a parallel passage to the Great Commission, Jesus says,

> These miraculous signs will accompany those who believe: They will cast out demons in my name, and they will speak in new languages. They will be able to handle snakes with safety, and if they drink anything poisonous, it won't hurt them. They will be able to place their hands on the sick, and they will be healed.
>
> Mark 16:17–18

These signs point to Jesus and follow those who believe. The Greek word for *believe* is *pisteúō*, which means "faith, to trust in, to be fully convinced, to rely on." It is much more than a head knowledge; it is believing from the heart. It expresses a personal trust and reliance that produces obedience to Jesus.

Jesus was constantly calling His disciples to have faith. In Mark 11:22–24, Jesus challenged them this way:

> Have faith in God. I tell you the truth, you can say to this mountain, "May you be lifted up and thrown into the sea," and it will happen. But you must really believe it will happen and have no doubt in your heart. I tell you, you can pray for anything, and if you believe that you've received it, it will be yours.

When I was studying renewal theology with Dr. Randy Clark, I learned that the phrase "have faith *in* God" could be translated "have faith *of* God." In 1 Corinthians 12:9, this is called a "gift of faith" or "great faith." It's the God-type of faith that moves mountains and performs miracles.

In the passage from Mark 11, we see a few simple instructions from Jesus:

1. Have faith *in/of* God.
2. Declare (speak to mountains or obstacles).
3. Believe it will happen.
4. Have no doubt in your heart.
5. Pray for anything.
6. Believe you have received it.
7. Forgive others from the heart.

That last instruction actually comes from Mark 11:25, which adds an element that points to the heart. In this dynamic, power-packed verse, Jesus is activating the faith of the disciples by telling them, "But when you are praying, first forgive anyone you are holding a grudge against, so that your Father in heaven will forgive your sins, too." In the midst of praying, declaring, and believing, Jesus warns about unforgiveness hiding in the heart. A heart filled with bitterness, holding a grudge against others, will not be able to see the miracles God has ready. Jesus instructs the disciples:

1. Right away, first forgive while you are praying.
2. Forgive anyone you are holding a grudge against.
3. Receive God's forgiveness from heaven for *your sin*.

It's so easy to see the sin of others, but the finger of God in this passage is pointing to the sin of unforgiveness that may be hidden in our own hearts.

A Pure Heart Sees God

Your heart condition affects whether prayers of faith are answered. If your heart is filled with bitterness, selfish ambition, or materialism, you will not see all that God has for you.

Jesus talked about this truth in the Sermon on the Mount: "Blessed [anticipating God's presence, spiritually mature] are the pure in heart [those with integrity, moral courage, and godly character], for they will see God" (Matthew 5:8 AMP).

We are blessed with God's presence when we come to Him with a pure heart. As a mature believer, you are called to walk in spiritual integrity, moral courage, and godly character.

The purity in your heart is a measure for seeing the things of God in fullness. Let's shift our focus here, however, and look at two types of faith: the faith that endures, and the faith that moves mountains.

Two Types of Faith

Enduring faith and a *gift of faith* are two wings that carry divine revelation. *Enduring faith* is used to describe the type of faith in the life of a disciple that steadily grows through intimacy with Jesus. It is developed in our character over a lifetime of intimate connection and obedience to Him.

This type of faith is seen through the life of every disciple, beginning at salvation. Enduring faith continues to grow by degrees of faithfulness to God and consistently walking in the fruit of the Holy Spirit. It also develops through suffering. As a sculptor, God uses a hammer to break hard places in marble-like souls. He uses a chisel to carve magnificent attributes into the character of men and women. He uses a grinder to smooth rough edges off of mental attitudes.

God develops deep and lasting faith inside us throughout our lifetime. Because enduring faith is widely understood in the Body of Christ, I want to focus more on the *gift of faith*. First, let's define what it is. The *gift of faith*, or we can call it *mountain-moving faith*, is a divinely inspired confidence that often produces healings or miracles. This gift unlocks power from heaven to heal the sick and perform miracles. When you have a gift of faith, fear is completely absent. It is one of the three "power gifts" mentioned together in 1 Corinthians 12: *gift of faith*, *gifts of healing*, and *working of miracles*. These three power gifts often work together to bring heaven's power to earth by using humble vessels who believe. Both the mountain-moving faith Jesus talks about in Mark 11:22–25 and the gift of faith in 1 Corinthians 12:9 are the kind of faith that produces healing and miracles.

The source of a gift of faith is divine revelation. A disciple cannot create a gift of faith. A gift of faith comes from listening intently to the voice of God and boldly obeying His voice. God initiates a gift of faith, and a believer receives the imparted gift and acts on what has been imparted.

This mountain-moving gift of faith requires believers to lay hold of God's advancing Kingdom that Jesus described in Matthew 11:12 (NRSV): "From the days of John the Baptist until now the kingdom of heaven has suffered violence, and the violent take it by force." God's Kingdom is advancing forcefully. The question is, Will disciples of Jesus Christ lay hold of heaven's power?

In order for Christians to advance the Kingdom of God today, disciples need to embrace both *enduring faith* and a supernatural kind of faith—*a gift of faith*. A well-rounded theology of faith needs to include the belief that miracles are for today.

Experiencing the Gift of Faith

I have experienced this *gift of faith*, or *mountain-moving faith*, on a number of occasions. The first time was when my daughter Sarah was born at home with the cord wrapped around her neck. Sarah was blue, but as I held her I spoke her middle name over her, "*Faith, Faith, Faith*," and she recovered quickly and completely.

The next miracle was needed for my own life. The afterbirth refused to come out, even with every attempt the midwives made. After I had lost a great deal of blood, the midwives were preparing for an ambulance to come take me to the emergency room.

(They estimated my blood loss at 2,500 cc's!) With my remaining strength, however, I stood leaning on both midwives, and with authority from heaven I shouted at the top of my voice, "In the name of Jesus, I command you to come out!"

At that moment, the afterbirth fell out of my body. I didn't need to go to the emergency room, either. Other than one fainting spell, I recovered quickly. It became a picture to me of the spiritual battles each of us face in our personal lives.

Another time I sensed *mountain-moving faith* was as an associate pastor and principal of an academy. We had seen an unusual amount of rainfall at the end of one school year and had needed to postpone our field day three times. On the last possible day we could hold the event, I was driving with my children to the event location when the secretary called me from there. "Should we cancel?" she asked.

"No. Gather all the children and parents under the pavilion and wait for me to arrive," I told her.

I arrived and saw that the parents looked miserable and ready to go home. I didn't focus on them. I jumped on the picnic table and began to preach from Mark 4:35–41.

"Kids, come close," I told the students. I looked into their expectant eyes and was filled with childlike faith. "Do you remember the story of when Jesus was in the boat with His disciples and they had a storm?"

"Yes!" they all shouted. They loved stories.

"The rain fell and the waves crashed!" I shouted. I had the kids move back and forth like the moving of the sea.

"The waves became bigger and began to fill the ship. The disciples thought they were going to die. Turn to your neighbor and say, 'We're all going to die!'" The kids acted out the scene of the crashing waves and the fear in the disciples.

"But Jesus wasn't scared. He rested His head on the pillow." I had the kids all lean their head in their hands, acting as though they were sleeping.

"'Jesus, don't you care that we're all going to drown?' the disciples asked." I had the kids tell each other, "We're all going to drown!"

"But Jesus wasn't scared. He stood up and rebuked the storm: 'Quiet. Be still.' Then He turned to the disciples and asked, 'Why are you so afraid? Why don't you have faith?'"

Then I asked, "Kids, do you have faith that if we command the rain to stop in Jesus' name, it will happen?"

"Yes!" they all shouted again.

Believe me, I know this sounds crazy. But in that moment, I had a *gift of faith* in my heart, and a calm knowing that we could command this rain to go.

"In the name of Jesus, we rebuke the rain and command it to go. In Your name, Jesus, we believe You can do this."

After this simple prayer, the rain stopped and we set up for field day. By the end of the day the sun came out, and a rainbow came out that reminded the kids of God's promise. The faith level of the kids, the parents, and the teachers increased. From that time forward, the entire academy prayed with greater faith.

Every time I sense a gift of faith in my heart, I see an increase in miracles. I had a gift of faith the day the Lord healed my physical heart and my broken heart. I had a gift of faith when praying for others with heart defects that were healed. I had a gift of faith when my thyroid was miraculously healed in Brazil. Whenever I'm filled with a gift of faith, there is a calm knowing in my heart and bold action to follow God's prompting.

Faith to Raise the Dead

After I preached at Orlando International Worship Center in Florida, Pastors Paul and Evelyn Williams took me out to eat. Paul and Evelyn serve as senior pastors there. We sat around the dinner table, talking about the miracles of God that we had seen. Evelyn told me this story about a gift of faith:

I was taught to believe that God does miracles today. I grew up seeing God do amazing healings and cast out demons at revival meetings. One morning, a friend of ours came to my back door. Crying, this grief-stricken parent sobbed, "My son is dead!"

As my friend told me the details, faith began to grow in my heart. This son had been riding his bike to church and was hit by a car. Now he was lying in the median of the road.

I felt an unction from the Holy Spirit. I had a gift of faith. I grabbed my coat and immediately drove to the accident. The body of the boy, covered by a coat, had been lying on the road for 45 minutes. A doctor had been driving the car that had hit the boy, and this doctor had pronounced him dead at the scene. The ambulance was there, but they were waiting on the medical examiner before they moved the body.

"Put the boy in the ambulance and let's go to the hospital," I told them. I couldn't believe how bold I was. I knew it was the Spirit leading me.

"He's already dead," the ambulance worker said.

"You need to take the boy to the hospital," I persisted.

The workers grudgingly agreed to carry the body to the ambulance, and they began driving to the hospital without a siren or lights. I got into the ambulance, crawled over the seat, and placed my hands on the boy's dead body. I began to pray.

"If you can hear me, make a sound," I told him. At first, there was no response. I persisted, "If you can hear me, make a sound."

The boy began to groan out loud. When the skeptical ambulance driver heard the boy's moans, he put on the sirens and raced to the hospital. The boy lived into adulthood to tell the story of being raised from the dead.

As Evelyn looked back at this miracle that God did through her, she said, "I had faith that God would work this miracle. I knew in my heart that God would raise this boy from the dead."

Faith Is the Currency of Heaven

The faith of believers is beautiful in the sight of God: "And without faith it is impossible to please God, for whoever would approach him must believe that he exists and that he rewards those who seek him" (Hebrews 11:6 NRSV).

When the disciples had trouble calming the storm that Jesus slept through, Jesus not only rebuked the storm, but He also rebuked the disciples, asking them, "Where is your faith?" (Luke 8:25). Jesus was calling the disciples into a miraculous lifestyle where they, too, could command the natural elements to obey their words.

Jesus called His disciples to walk in mountain-moving faith. He put them in situations where He expected them to do what was impossible. When faced with the insurmountable problem of feeding five thousand, Jesus pressed the disciples into the miraculous. The disciples wanted to send the crowd away, but Jesus said, "They need not go away; you give them something to eat" (Mathew 14:16 NRSV). Then He modeled what to do: "Taking the five loaves and the two fish, he looked up to heaven, and blessed and broke the loaves, and gave them to the disciples, and the disciples gave them to the crowds" (verse 19 NRSV).

Jesus put the bread in the hands of the disciples, and they miraculously fed the people. *The miracle of multiplication happened as the disciples served.* Jesus called His disciples to work miracles. He was demonstrating how to walk in this kind of faith. It was a manifestation of a grace gift of faith that came from heaven.

I have heard of the miracle of multiplication happening numerous times on the mission field. One day, I saw it happen in front of my eyes. The secretary from New Song Christian Academy came to me with a practical problem: "We prepared a spaghetti dinner for two hundred, but there are five hundred people here. What should we do?"

I looked around at the standing room only crowd at our spring play, listened to Jesus in my heart, and walked across the parking lot to the next building, into the kitchen. I reached my hand over the spaghetti dishes and prayed, *Jesus, I thank You for what You have provided. Bless each one who is here. I pray that You would multiply what we have so that everyone has enough to eat, with leftovers to spare. I thank You, Lord. In Jesus' name, Amen.*

I instructed the team to serve the food and believe that God would multiply it. Not only did we have enough to serve everyone, but we had food left over. I didn't feel any stress; I felt a calm faith, knowing that Jesus provides.

Activate Your Faith

The moment you made Jesus Christ the master of your life, receiving Him as Lord and Savior, you began your walk of faith. Romans 12:3 (NKJV) tells us that every believer has been given a measure of faith: "For I say, through the grace given to me, to everyone who is among you, not to think of himself more highly than he ought to think, but to think soberly, as God has dealt to each one a measure of faith." I love how The Message Bible says it:

> I'm speaking to you out of deep gratitude for all that God has given me, and especially as I have responsibilities in relation to you. Living then, as every one of you does, in pure grace, it's important that you not misinterpret yourselves as people who are bringing this goodness to God. No, God brings it all to you. The only accurate way to understand ourselves is by what God is and by what he does for us, not by what we are and what we do for him.

It's all about Jesus. All the glory, honor, and praise go to Him. Isn't it amazing that He wants to use you and me to advance His Kingdom?

Let's close this chapter by activating our faith through prayer. Pray this out loud:

Jesus,
it's all about You.
I pray that You would help me
stir up the faith You have given me.
Give me "enduring faith" that stands the test of time.
Help me fellowship with You in suffering,
having faith that I will also
share in Your resurrection.

Jesus,
help me see You for who You are.
You are the same yesterday, today, and forever.
You are the one who heals the sick,
casts out demons, and raises the dead.
I'm humbled and grateful that You want to use me
to accomplish these great works of faith.
I ask that You increase my awareness of the times
when You are imparting "mountain-moving faith."
Give me calm confidence and boldness
to work wonders for Your glory.
In Your name I pray, Amen.

eleven

Stand

Persevering for Divine Healing

Lauri Carnahan is a wife, a mom, and a grandma. She has served as an educator, a coach, and an administrator at a Christian school. Dave Carnahan, her husband, has been a businessman and serves as an elder at Grabill Missionary Church. Lauri Carnahan had this to say in a *Healing Rain* podcast interview about her journey of persevering for her healing:

> I married my high school sweetheart. We had three children and were busy building a life and business. We faced a significant challenge in our marriage when my husband had an affair, and we needed to forgive each other and get our relationship on a solid path. Then we had our fourth child, and not only was Dave leading our family business, but I was also in education and coaching. We had a busy but beautiful life together.
>
> Dave and I joined a large group from our church on a mission trip to Houston, Texas, where we cleaned up after Hurricane Harvey's devastation in 2018. I woke up on Valentine's Day during

that mission trip with a pain in my right eye. It felt like an irritant, but it continued to get worse. A few days later, when I was home, I went to an eye doctor, who immediately sent me to a specialist. I was first diagnosed with optic neuritis; then they wondered if I had multiple sclerosis.

How can I be losing my vision? I wondered. *I don't even feel sick.* Finally, I was diagnosed with an autoimmune disease called MOG (myelin oligodendrocyte glycoprotein). The MOG antibody disease causes inflammation in the optic nerve, but can also cause inflammation in the spinal cord, brain, and brainstem.

I was so frightened. I couldn't see even 10 percent out of that eye. I knew it was a possibility that I could go completely blind. I always seek the Lord for a word each year. In 2018, my word was *Focus*.

I had been the picture of health as an athlete. The MOG issue was a real shock to everyone. My husband was amazing and always gave me his arm to guide me as we walked. He was very attentive and helped me daily. My children were frightened, but they inspired me to walk through my healing journey with faith.

God, I want to do this well, I prayed. *Help me walk through this time trusting You and giving You glory. Help my family be strengthened in their faith.*

I also had the opportunity to share with my church family and my neighborhood Bible study group. I wanted to be a witness of my faith in Jesus as my healer. I concentrated on putting God first in my journey.

It was helpful being diagnosed, because I could begin my healing process. I was anointed with oil by the elders in my church, who prayed and believed with me for healing. Jesus is a miracle worker, and prayer is the place to begin.

At my lowest moment, I was seeing well in my right eye again, but then I began to lose vision in my left eye. I panicked. I cried out to God, saying, *God, I know that You have a good plan for my life. I know that You love me. I know that I'm Your daughter. I know that You are writing a beautiful story. Jesus, I'm scared. Can You show me that You're here?*

I got up, walked to my bedroom, and heard God say, *You can trust Me.*

This was a turning point for me, anchoring my trust in God. As I researched my condition, I found out one of the issues I could work on was stress. Reducing my stress became a goal for me. I also realized that the earlier trauma in my marriage had also impacted me, and I needed to continue healing in that arena. I began to see my patterns that had contributed to the challenge in our marriage, and I repented of my part. God healed our marriage, and it is more vital every day.

As I worshiped at God's throne, I could rest and give my anxiety to the Lord. I meditated on 1 Peter 5:7 [AMP]: "Casting all your cares [all your anxieties, all your worries, and all your concerns, once and for all] on Him, for He cares about you [with deepest affection, and watches over you very carefully]." I knew I needed to cast away my cares and rest in Him. I needed to give Him my anxious thoughts and past trauma. I needed to slow down and decrease my stress.

I learned to abide by Jesus and be honest with my emotions. Sometimes, I just needed to say, *God, I'm so scared right now.* I needed to renew my mind every day. I meditated on Romans 12:2 (VOICE): "Do not allow this world to mold you in its own image. Instead, be transformed from the inside out by renewing your mind. As a result, you will be able to discern what God wills and whatever God finds good, pleasing, and complete."

God has done a miracle in my eyes, and He has healed me from going completely blind. He has also healed my body and taught me to take better care of the temple of God as I rest in Him and trust Him. I can now see very well physically because I focused on Him.

Create a Safe Place to Heal

Jesus is our healer. The healing of our heart impacts our physical body. We need to create a safe place to heal while in the middle of the journey.

Remember how I said that when I was going into double knee replacement God told my heart that *the miracle is in the surgery*? I knew I would be experiencing incredible pain as my knees fully healed, and God gave me a song to meditate on called "You Make Me Brave" by Amanda Cook.[1] We need to focus on God's Word and believe that He cares. He hears your prayers and the secret cries of your heart.

One day, I was talking and praying with a friend whom I mentioned in chapter 2, Elizabeth Reed. She is a functional nutritionist who has helped many people struggling with autoimmune issues and chronic inflammation find a healing pathway that's right for them. When I told her my next book was on healing, her response was, "I think your next book is going to be about suffering." I just laughed and thought, *No one is going to pick up and buy a book about suffering.* Yet suffering is in the valley on our way to healing. God's healing doesn't stop on this earth. In eternity, we get brand-new heavenly bodies. In eternity, He wipes away every tear of suffering.

When there's a healing process, we are changed in the middle of the journey. God gives us other believers to encourage us with His hope. There are also three things we can focus on when we experience a longer healing journey:

1. *Worship:* This helps you focus on Jesus as your healer.
2. *Prayer:* This digs the well of intimacy with Jesus.
3. *Meditating on God's Word:* What you focus on, you will magnify.

Let's put these three vital elements of your healing journey into action: Begin by choosing a worship song. One that I'm worshiping with today is "Jesus, the Healer" with Lindy Cofer, Elyssa Smith, and the Circuit Riders.[2] Plan to take an extended time for prayer as you meditate on the following healing Scriptures.

DIVING DEEPER
IN GOD'S WORD

The Hebrew word for *meditating* is *hagah*, which means "to meditate, mourn, speak, imagine, study, mutter, roar, and talk." The Hebrew way of meditation is the opposite of emptying your mind. A biblical meditation perspective is to contemplate Scripture and speak or declare its words out loud. You enter into God's presence in communion with the face of God by praying His Word back to Him. You may do this while walking back and forth, or bowing the way they do at the Wailing Wall in Jerusalem. One of the places this Hebrew word for meditating is used is in Joshua 1:8 (VOICE):

> Let the words from the book of the law be always on your lips. Meditate on them day and night so that you may be careful to live by all written in it. If you do, as you make your way through this world, you will prosper and always find success.

In the following exercise, meditate on each of the healing Scriptures just ahead by taking these three steps:

1. *Pray the verse out loud* from a Bible version you like, and then go back and *pray it again, making it personal this time*. I'll use Joshua 1:8 as an example to show you how:

> *Lord, imprint Your written and spoken Word on my heart and on my lips. Day and night, I pray that I would wake up thinking about Your Word so that I*

149

*would live by everything You've written. God, You've
given me an instruction manual to live by in this world
so I can prosper in every area of my life, including my
health and finances. Thank You, God, that You are my
success.*

2. *Imagine yourself doing what the verse says.* I picture
myself with power-packed words coming out of my
heart like vibrant red energy and moving to my lips
as words. I imagine mountains moving as I speak the
Word of God in faith (see Mark 11:22–24).

3. *Add descriptive wording as you pray.* For example,

*Lord, help me engage in study, meditation, and speak-
ing out Your Word with my entire being. Give me a
daily revelation of Your divine Word. Help me not to get
off track, but to meditate on, ponder, and imagine Your
Word day and night. Anoint me to put into practice
everything that Your Word says. Every step gives me
strength and courage, and prospers and heals me in my
heart, relationships, and finances. Help me celebrate
daily the success that You bring in small and big ways
as I intimately walk with You.*

I hope you enjoyed this example. Now meditate on the
following Scriptures yourself, taking the three steps I just
described. You can do this exercise verbally or write out
the Scriptures as prayers. (With some of these passages,
I have included more examples for you of personalizing
the verses.)

You shall serve [only] the LORD your God, and He shall bless your bread and water. I will also remove sickness from among you. No one shall suffer miscarriage or be barren in your land; I will fulfill the number of your days.

Exodus 23:25–26 AMP

Yet it was our suffering he carried, our pain and distress, our sick-to-the-soul-ness. We just figured that God had rejected him, that God was the reason he hurt so badly. But he was hurt because of us; he suffered so. Our wrongdoing wounded and crushed him. He endured the breaking that made us whole. The injuries he suffered became our healing.

Isaiah 53:4–5 VOICE

The New King James Version puts Isaiah 53:5 this way: ". . . by His stripes we are healed."

We read in Acts 10:38 (VOICE) how God anointed Jesus as uniquely chosen to go around doing good and healing the sick and suffering:

You know God identified Jesus as the uniquely chosen One by pouring out the Holy Spirit on Him, by empowering Him. You know Jesus went through the land doing good for all and healing all who were suffering under the oppression of the evil one, for God was with Him.

Now identify yourself with this verse to make it personal:

You know God anointed me, [insert your name], as uniquely chosen by pouring out the Holy Spirit on me, by empowering me. You know I, [name], go around doing good and healing those suffering under the oppression of the evil one, for God is with me, [name].

Jesus told Peter in Matthew 16:19 (VOICE),

Peter, I give you the keys to the kingdom of heaven. Whatever you bind on earth will be bound in heaven, and whatever you loose on earth will be loosed in heaven.

Here's an example of how to make this verse bold and personal:

[Insert your name], I give you the keys to the Kingdom of heaven. Whatever you bind on earth, [insert your name], will be bound in heaven, and whatever you loose on earth, [name], will be loosed in heaven.

Now be even more specific:

In heaven, there is no sickness or disease; my Jesus has already bound it. Today, with Your anointing and power, I bind every form of illness and disease in my body [list specific diseases] and in the bodies of my family and loved ones. . . . I bind autoimmune diseases [name them: Hashimoto's thyroiditis, alopecia areta, etc.]. I loose health, healing, and wholeness. I command my body to come into alignment with God's Word. . . .

Now identify with these two passages by making them personal yourself and praying them out loud:

My child, pay attention to what I say. Listen carefully to my words. Don't lose sight of them. Let them penetrate deep into your heart, for they bring life to those who find them, and healing to their whole body.

Proverbs 4:20–22

Never doubt God's mighty power to work in you and accomplish all this. He will achieve infinitely more than your greatest request, your most unbelievable dream, and exceed your wildest imagination! He will outdo them all, for his miraculous power constantly energizes you.

Ephesians 3:20 TPT

What's your "unbelievable dream" for your health? Never doubt God's mighty power to work in you to accomplish it.

Keep going with praying and personalizing this final passage:

O my soul, come, praise the Eternal with all that is in me—body, emotions, mind, and will—every part of who I am—praise His holy name. O my soul, come, praise the Eternal; sing a song from a grateful heart; sing and never forget all the good He has done. Despite all your many offenses, He forgives and releases you. More than any doctor, He heals your diseases. He reaches deep into the pit to deliver you from death. He crowns you with unfailing love and compassion like a king. When your soul is famished and withering, He fills you with good and beautiful things, satisfying you as long as you live. He makes you strong like an eagle, restoring your youth.

Psalm 103:1–5 VOICE

Healing Moments
FOR YOUR HEART AND HEALTH

◆

God heals your heart and your body. Let me ask you a few questions. Let the Holy Spirit search your heart for honest answers, and write down whatever He brings to mind.

- Is there an issue in your life that causes you to be afraid? When Lauri shared her fear with God, He said, "You can trust Me." What is God saying to you? Write it down.

- Do you need healing for a physical issue? Take a moment to journal with God about your need for healing. Now take a moment to listen and write down what He says to you. Are you frustrated by how long it is taking to experience physical healing? If so, take a moment to journal your frustration to Jesus. Let Him know how you are feeling. But don't stop there! Listen to what He says to you and write it down.

- Remember how I wrote in my journal that God said He was healing my thyroid? It took a year and a half for my body to manifest the physical healing. I'm glad I wrote what I believed God was saying to me. There is often a time lapse between the moment God speaks to us and its physical manifestation. Close your time with Jesus voicing these words out loud.

Jesus, name above all names,
You're my wonderful savior,

You're my healer,
You're my Lord.

You're not bound by time,
You're eternal,
You're not frustrated by delays,
You see the end from the beginning.

Today I choose to not grow weary.
I will continue to believe and speak your word.
I embrace the mystery of your kingdom.
Your kingdom is now, and not yet.

Thank you, Jesus.
In Your name I pray, Amen.

twelve

Wholeness

Immersed in the Father's Love

Kimberly Stokes specializes in connection. Today, she hosts the *Imagine More Podcast* and serves as a Connect Coach to help people find connections with God, self, and others. She talked in a *Healing Rain* podcast interview about her own pathway to connecting with God:

> In my family of origin there were many expectations, so I grew up feeling an unspoken pressure to be perfect. As a junior in high school, I began to struggle with anorexia, and this battle continued throughout college. Eventually, I became a complete control freak. On the outside I looked perfect, but my shame was masked in deep-rooted perfectionism and academic success. I recognized that I had an eating disorder, but I wouldn't admit it to anyone else because that would shatter my facade of perfection.
>
> In my senior year of college, as I finished a practicum at a Christian counseling center, I deeply encountered the love of God, and He gently exposed wounds in my heart that He wanted

to heal. After that, I began to experience the love of the Father in ways I never dreamt possible. And this healing journey continued as I worked on my master's degree in counseling.

The Father began to expose performance mindsets that kept me in bondage, and His tangible love eventually led me into deep and lasting freedom. It was a long process, but proved a pathway to greater depths of intimacy with God. As the Father consistently poured His affection on me, I would receive His love daily. Eventually, His devotion and love penetrated the deepest parts of my heart and emotions.

On my journey to freedom from anorexia, perfectionism, and shame, the Father anchored my heart in my true identity as His child. Receiving His affection brought fresh revelation in my spirit that I was His daughter, and I didn't have to jump through hoops or perform for Him. His love was constant and had nothing to do with my performance. How freeing!

Being set free from perfectionism and anorexia was a life-changing experience as God moved biblical truths from cognitive constructs to experiential realities in my life based on His vast, unconditional love. As He consistently lavished His affection on me, He slowly and steadily healed my heart, mind, and emotions.

Experiencing the Father as a really good dad was a huge part of my healing journey. He told me repeatedly, *Child, it's My delight to love you. It's My joy to forgive you when you least deserve it.* And I was marked by His affection. I felt His presence every day as He whispered His words of love throughout that long season of healing. I was genuinely wrecked and undone by the Father's love.

Several years later, when I became a mom, I wanted my kids to "taste and see" the love of the Father through me, so I practiced being vulnerable with God and dependent on the Holy Spirit in the many messy moments of family life. When my children were little and throwing a fit, I would listen for the Father's voice and ask Him, *What's going on right now, Lord?* I learned to listen to Him at the moment so I could say what He said and do what He was doing.

I remember one time when our daughter was having a tantrum and the Lord whispered, *Get down on your knees and open your arms to her.* So I reluctantly followed His instruction, got on my knees, and opened my arms—and my daughter's anger melted away as she began to cry and ran into my arms for comfort.

Since encountering the love of the Father, my priority in life has become to receive from Him. All the fullness of Christ is available moment by moment if we'll simply open our hearts to receive from Him. When I lack love, grace, or patience in a situation, I lean into Him because He is my abundant sufficiency. He covers our gaps, and there's no lack in Him. We need to stay connected to His heart.

My life was radically changed as God slowly freed me from anorexia and healed my wounds from childhood. He freed me from perfectionism, from being an overachiever, and He obliterated all my shame. The tangible love of the Father was truly my lifeline and source of healing.

The pathway to intimacy with God is through our vulnerability and need for Him. As we honestly position our hearts before Him, He will lavish His affection upon us. And the more we receive His love, the more healing He brings to our hearts, lives, and relationships. I'm so grateful that the love of our Father is more than enough. His arms and heart are open wide, ready to comfort and lavish us with His affection.[1]

The Problem of an Orphan Heart

Kimberly Stokes was completely healed of anorexia, a potentially life-threatening disorder, by the healing of her heart. The turning point of her healing journey was when she encountered the Father's love. We live on an orphan planet that desperately needs the unconditional love of Father God. Since humanity's fall in the Garden of Eden, we have blamed others for our pain and have been striving to please God.

An orphan heart feels abandoned, rejected, misunderstood, and even entitled. For many, this begins with a father wound or a mother wound. Someone in authority over you did not give you the security your heart needed, so your identity got entangled with performance. Do any of the following sound like a fleshly pattern you've observed in yourself or others?

- Performing to please
- Striving to achieve
- Perfecting to control
- Medicating to escape

We only find security, rest, and peace nestled into a love relationship with the Father, made possible for each of us by the atoning sacrifice of the Son and the prompting of the Holy Spirit. We step into the domain of fear whenever we step out of a love motivation in our hearts. In the domain of fear, we are operating outside the Father's provision: "For everything in the world—the lust of the flesh, the lust of the eyes, and the pride of life—comes not from the Father but from the world" (1 John 2:16 NIV).

Our Father in heaven has already provided everything we need for life, love, relationships, and provision. However, when we step out of the Father's realm and into the world's realm, our natural desires move us toward

- the lust of the flesh (drug addictions, sex addictions, fornication, adultery, etc.),
- the lust of the eyes (greed for money, material possessions, appearances, etc.), and
- the pride of life (in a world system built on pride, external success, achievement, etc.).

One way or another, we're trying to fill the void in our hearts. We feel entitled to things. An orphan feels as though "People owe me." We are trying to medicate our pain, mend our hearts, or counsel our own souls. We strive to get love in all the wrong places, forgetting we've already been given the Father's unconditional love.

No Longer an Orphan

Leif Hetland is an author and the founder and president of Global Mission Awareness. He has led over one million Muslims to Jesus through sharing the Father's love and forgiveness. When Leif was a Baptist pastor in Norway and was translating for Randy Clark, he received a supernatural impartation for healing and miracles. Leif remembers,

> It was the humility of Randy Clark that touched my heart. I thought, *If God could do this for him, God can do it for me.* He had shared about his weakness, so it opened my heart to share my weakness. So when the prayer time came, my heart was open to receive.
>
> As Randy ministered, people were falling down in the Spirit. When he came to me, he said, "You are a bulldozer; you are going to go into the darkest areas of the world, where the Gospel has never been before, and make a way where there is no way." In the next moment, I was down, shaking with fire and electricity. As a Baptist pastor, I received the Holy Spirit's baptism.
>
> The Holy Spirit was now not just *in* me; the Holy Spirit *was upon* me. Six months later, I was in the Middle East. I was in one of the darkest places, at a crusade with twenty thousand people. I saw lame people walk, blind eyes see, deaf ears open, and cancer disappear. I could see women behind their veils weeping as the presence and power of Jesus filled the place. Since then, I've never been the same.
>
> That began a new transformation in my life, a new calling, a new fire. Most of this ministry was done out of an urgency and

gratitude to Jesus. For the next five years, I was in fifty countries, seeing half a million people saved and three hundred thousand people healed.

On the inside, I had a black hole in my soul. I had an orphan heart—all of what I was doing was *for* God. I didn't know how to live *from* God. I was motivated by being a *servant* rather than a *son*. On the inside of my heart, there was still something missing. For a long time, I didn't know what it was. Now I know it was a *love deficiency*.

When there is a *love deficiency*, there is a *God deficiency*. You are looking for love in the wrong places. I knew Jesus, the Holy Spirit, and everything about Papa God, but I didn't really know the Father. I was looking for affirmation. On the inside, I wanted to please Him. I didn't realize I already pleased Him.

I had become an achiever. With orphans, you get value in what you are doing instead of who you are. I didn't know we were living in this orphan world, because everyone I knew was operating in this orphan system. As orphans, you *compete* with one another. Sons and daughters *complete* one another. I had so many break-throughs in ministry, but my body was breaking down.

At this point in my life, even though I saw amazing miracles on the mission field, I was in a lot of pain. I had a broken neck and a broken back. After going through surgery, I was in a body cast.

One day, I was sitting in a wheelchair and my baby daughter was sitting on my lap. It started to rain, and I said to God, *I'm not able to do anything any longer. I can't be a husband, I can't be a father, I can't be a provider, I can't be a pastor or a leader. I don't know how to do anything any longer. My body is broken, my spirit is broken, I'm rejected. . . .*

I went through a major crisis. But that crisis was really a bless-ing. It was at the darkest moment of my life that I had a baptism of love experience. I was in Melbourne, Florida, with Jack Taylor, who later became a spiritual father to me. There were only eighty or ninety leaders in the room. Dennis Jernigan was playing the piano, and he said, "Leif, I have a song for you. It is a Daddy's song of Papa God's love for you."

Suddenly, a wave of Papa God's love came over me, and then wave after wave of His love. The healing stream of God's love took me all the way back to when I was a baby in my mother's womb, where I had felt fear; God's perfect love took away that fear. It took me to when I was twelve years old and had struggled with shame, and His love covered me. It took me to the rejection I had felt as a Baptist pastor; His love came in.

I was the orphan who was trying to please God; His love came in, and it didn't stop. It was waves and waves of His love. I was melted in the Father's love. I lay on the floor and wept for over two hours. I was overwhelmed by His voice. I heard an audible voice from heaven that said, *Leif, you are Mine. You are My beloved son. I love you. I am well pleased with you.*

At that moment, something went into the root of my life and it broke. I was changed. I was healed, transformed, and set free! I meditated on God's words to me and realized, *I'm Papa's son. He loves me. He delights in me. He likes me. He's pleased with me. I don't have to do any of these things any longer.* I remembered the verse "So if the Son sets you free, you will be free indeed" [John 8:36 NIV]. I became free that day. Before then, Islam was a *problem*; now it was a *promise*. Sickness and disease were a problem, and now they are a promise. There was a fundamental paradigm change when I received the baptism of love. I know I had lenses of love. I was wearing *SON* glasses now.

I now had a vision of the Father. All I had to do is what the Father was doing. All I say is what I hear the Father say. My ministry changed. My life changed. My marriage changed. It started a transformation that continues today. Being baptized with the Father's love started a movement that created a tsunami wave of love.[2]

Leif's love for the people he is reaching for Jesus touches my heart. He sees the promise of God for each person who presently embraces Islam, or who struggles with illness. He has walked with his Good Shepherd through the valleys of sickness and disease to find intimacy with Jesus, and the promise of healing—if not in this world, then in heaven.

Meditation Magnifies

I was teaching a systematic theology class for Life School of Ministry and had assigned an additional book for reading by A.W. Tozer called *The Attributes of God*. As the students and I were taking a journey into the Father heart of God, His holy presence came into the room. The fear of God rested on each one as we began to fall prostrate before Him with tearful repentance, as well as humble adoration. We had simply been meditating on who the Father is when He entered the room and ministered His presence to us.

What you meditate on, you magnify. Let's take time to meditate on the nature of God. Let's meditate on who Abba is:

1. *He is infinite.* His measureless love is absolute and everlasting. His affection for you as His child is unending. His promises over your life are immense. His love is perpetual and enduring.

2. *He is boundless.* His vast domain is without comprehension, and yet He knows all the hairs on your head; your name is written in the palm of His hand.

3. *He is good.* He is flawless and perfect. He is merciful and kindhearted. He is authentic, real, and true. Everything He does is for your benefit.

4. *He is blameless.* Everything about His nature is just and righteous. He is holy and awesome. He loved you so much that He sent Jesus to be a bridge for you so you could have an intimate relationship with Him.

5. *He is merciful.* He is compassionate and forgiving. He doesn't treat you as your sin deserves; He lifts you up and heals your heart.

6. *He is gracious.* He is approachable, a Daddy who holds you in His lap. He is considerate of your hopes, dreams, and desires.

7. *He is always present.* He is universal in His love for every nation, every tribe worldwide. He is infinite. He is always there for you. He is in the intimate details of your life.
8. *He is indwelling.* He has chosen you as His temple. You have inherited His nature through Christ's intervention on the cross. He has sent the Holy Spirit to be your Advocate.

Jesus' Words about the Father

As you meditate on God's nature and attributes, also look at what Jesus said about the Father:

1. *He is trustworthy.* "Don't let your hearts be troubled. Trust in God, and trust also in me" (John 14:1).
2. *He is generous.* "There is more than enough room in my Father's home. If this were not so, would I have told you that I am going to prepare a place for you?" (John 14:2).
3. *He is approachable—through Jesus.* "I am the way, the truth, and the life. No one can come to the Father except through me" (John 14:6).
4. *He is the model.* "Anyone who has seen me has seen the Father!" (John 14:9).
5. *He gives divine instructions.* "I have not ever acted, and will not in the future act, on My own. I listen to the directions of the One who sent Me and act on these divine instructions. For this reason, My judgment is always fair and never self-serving. I'm committed to pursuing God's agenda and not My own" (John 5:30 VOICE).

Jesus came to show you the Father so you could be immersed in His love. As sons and daughters, we grow into maturity by first discovering our identity in Christ. Jesus Christ is the Anointed One who heals our internal wounds. Jesus always points us to the Father. When He came to earth, Jesus radically shifted people's perspective of who the Father is. As you see the Father rightly, you will begin to understand who you are as a son or daughter of God. Look at your access to the Father:

- You have full access to the Father.
- You can approach your Father with boldness.
- You are part of your Father's family.
- You carry your Father's name.
- You are established and endorsed by your Father.
- You are born into your position as your Father's child; it's not an earned position.
- You inherit all the promises of God.
- You can receive your Father's provision in all areas, at all times.

Out of our intimacy with the Father, we can live from our inheritance rather than toward it. This is how we step into our destiny. So many believers are frustrated over negative or hurtful words that have been spoken over them that they forget they're already betrothed to Jesus. They already have a covenant relationship with God as a son or a daughter.

As you are immersed in the Father's love, your mind, body, and heart will find true and everlasting healing. As you receive His healing, you become a healer to others. As you become fruitful, multiply, and walk in dominion on this earth, you bring glory and honor to your Father in heaven. His healing rain empowers you to

- reign with Christ in *endurance* (see Luke 22:28–30),
- reign with Christ in *humility* (see Matthew 5:3, 5),

- reign with Christ in *purity* (see Titus 2:1–5), and
- reign with Christ in *the love of truth* (see 2 Thessalonians 2:9–11).

Stepping into Your Joyful Call

When we encounter the love of the Father, it becomes a reality that shows us the depths of His love. We are completely forgiven. It takes no striving or performance. As we receive a baptism of His love, we find joy and contentment in walking with Him every day.

Every human being is made in the image of God, for the purpose of relationship. Part of our eternal design is to be in intimate fellowship with God. You are part of a chosen generation, a chosen race that recognizes God as Father, and recognizes the Son as King of kings and Lord of lords. You were born for royalty. God is the master artist, and you are His masterpiece (see Ephesians 2:10).

You have been designed by God to overflow with joy. The fullness of joy brings you everyday strength. Joy is your inheritance today. Step into your joyful call to be a son or daughter of God. Knowing your identity as His child anchors you to the heart of the Father.

Healing Moments

FOR YOUR HEART AND HEALTH

◆

- Meditate on *the nature of God*. (Remember that what you meditate on, you magnify.) Choose at least three of His attributes and write a prayer to Father God magnifying Him.

- Meditate on *your access to God*. Now write down your answer to this question: If you had all the money in the world and you knew you couldn't fail, what do you believe God would call you to do?

thirteen

Prevail

Embracing Time with Jesus

Gretchen Rodriguez is an author and the host of *The Breathing God Podcast*. She tells this encouraging story about taking time with God:

> When we get our eyes off of us and gaze at the one who loves us, He will lead us with His eyes. It's so important that our relationship with Him is solid inside of us. We need to find comfort in our love relationship with our Father in heaven.
>
> I was super busy when Covid hit and we were all quarantined. I heard the Lord say to me, *Can you just set everything aside? This is one of your most amazing seasons with Me.*
>
> I said to Him, *It doesn't feel very amazing; the world's going wacko. Lord, what is happening?*
>
> He said to me, *This is your Mary season; just come and sit at My feet.*
>
> *But, Lord, I have X, Y, Z that I have to do.*

He said to me, *Really, do you have to do it?* He said to me, *You've gotten too busy—slow down. You can choose to make this season chaotic, or you can choose to make this season your Mary moment.*

Slow Down and Take a Breath

The world would love for you to get too busy. Immersing yourself in Christ's love will help you find healing in your mind, your body, and your heart. You, too, can sit at Jesus' feet, as Mary did:

> As Jesus and his disciples were on their way, he came to a village where a woman named Martha opened her home to him. She had a sister called Mary, who sat at the Lord's feet listening to what he said. But Martha was distracted by all the preparations that had to be made. She came to him and asked, "Lord, don't you care that my sister has left me to do the work by myself? Tell her to help me!"
>
> "Martha, Martha," the Lord answered, "you are worried and upset about many things, but few things are needed—or indeed only one. Mary has chosen what is better, and it will not be taken away from her."
>
> Luke 10:38–42 NIV

Mary refused to be distracted; she chose intimacy with Jesus. She was at peace receiving from Him. Immersing yourself in Christ's love requires you to slow down and spend intimate time with Him.

Bold Faith and Quiet Trust

Disappointment and discouragement that linger in our hearts can be twisted by the enemy to cause us to fall into the temptation and sin of unbelief. Faith is the confidence that God is good and that He will be faithful to the end.

Bold faith brings your Father God great joy: "But without faith it is impossible to please Him, for he who comes to God must believe that He is, and that He is a rewarder of those who diligently seek Him" (Hebrews 11:6 NKJV). When you walk in faith, it pleases God. He is faithful in fulfilling His promises.

Healing Moments
FOR YOUR HEART AND HEALTH

◆

Think about what choosing intimacy with God will mean in your life, and ask yourself the following questions:

- Father, what areas in my life do You want me to let go of or lay down so that I can have more time for intimacy with You? Are there areas in my life that are a distraction?

- Father, in what areas in my life do You want me to embrace bold faith fully and believe You? (Be very specific, writing down the promises of God.)

◆

DIVING DEEPER
IN GOD'S WORD

Now take a moment, clear your mind, and breathe deeply. Meditate on the following verse, and ask yourself the questions that follow it:

> Since we first heard about you, we've kept you always in our prayers that you would receive the perfect knowledge of God's pleasure over your lives, making you reservoirs of every kind of wisdom and spiritual understanding.
>
> Colossians 1:9 TPT

- What does it mean that "you would receive the perfect knowledge of God's pleasure" over your life?
- How do we become "reservoirs of every kind of wisdom and spiritual understanding"?

Now read this verse in a different translation and make a comparison of the two versions:

> For this reason, since the day we heard it, we have not ceased praying for you and asking that you may be filled with the knowledge of God's will in all spiritual wisdom and understanding.
>
> Colossians 1:9 NRSV

Did you notice how one version says "knowledge of God's will" and the other says "knowledge of God's pleasure"? Most translations don't say "God's pleasure," as The Passion Translation does; they say "God's will." The Greek word comes from the root *thelema*, which can be translated as "pleasure," "desire," or "will."

I was praying with a young woman who wanted to know God's will for her life. She told me, "I have two good job opportunities in front of me, but I'm confused."

"What's causing the confusion?" I asked her. "What are you afraid of?"

She replied, "I'm afraid I will miss God. I'm afraid I will do something wrong."

Do you ever feel that way? Are you afraid you will miss God's will? If I meditate on all the things I need to do to please God, to be in the center of His will, it tends to trigger a performance mentality in me. However, if I meditate on how God has pleasure for me, or how He delights in me, it brings great joy and freedom to my heart. I feel a lightness in His presence. It's easier for me to make choices, because I'm starting from a place of security in Christ.

Meditate on this verse: "But even if we are faithless, he will still be full of faith, for he never wavers in his faithfulness to us!" (2 Timothy 2:13 TPT). Even if you are unfaithful, God will always be faithful to you. Your conduct and choices do not stop God's love. His love is constantly flowing from heaven. When you embrace His passion, it's like turning on the shower and getting in. You become immersed in healing rain!

From the foundation of the earth, God loved you. Your sin can harden *your heart* toward God. However, your sin doesn't harden *God's heart* toward you.

Now meditate on this verse: "For we are God's masterpiece. He has created us anew in Christ Jesus, so we can do the good things he planned for us long ago" (Ephesians 2:10). The Greek word *poiema* here is translated "workmanship" or "masterpiece." The context is that God is the great artist and you are His masterpiece. Or you could look at it as God being the great poet and you being His poetry, read to the world by your life. God is the master designer, and the world is His grand creation. Compare this version of the verse, and then answer the question that follows it:

> We have become his poetry, a re-created people that will fulfill the destiny he has given each of us, for we are joined to Jesus, the Anointed One. Even before we were born, God planned in advance our destiny and the good works we would do to fulfill it!
>
> Ephesians 2:10 TPT

- As you meditate on Ephesians 2:10, is the heart of the passage being joined with Christ, or is it performing to please Christ?

Whenever I think of destiny as a destination, it triggers a performance mentality in me. However, if I meditate on Jesus, the Anointed One, I simply need to receive the downpour of His love and divine empowerment in my life. His grace and anointing equip me to be who He created me to be. Embracing the journey with Jesus makes my life an adventure.

- Close your time in this chapter with a prayer. Concentrate on being connected and close to Jesus. Write down what you hear Him saying to you.

fourteen

Anointing to Heal

Soaking in His Presence

Bob Sorge is "the speaker who can't talk." His voice is reduced to a whisper because of a debilitating vocal injury he suffered over twenty years ago. In an interview with me on the *Healing Rain* podcast, Bob literally whispered this story:

> My voice is very small. In 1992, I was a pastor and worship leader in upstate New York. I developed an ulcer in my throat, next to my vocal cords. The ulcer was in the arytenoid cartilage, which is essential to vocal sound production. I had surgery that removed the ulcer but left me in chronic pain and decreased my voice capacity to a whisper.
>
> I was in the crisis of my life. What does a pastor do when he can't preach? What does a worship leader do when he can't sing? I have always had great faith in miracles, and now I was in a crisis of belief. I believe in the promises of God and that by Christ's stripes I am healed, but my healing hasn't come yet.

The fabric of who I am is that I believe in faith, healing, and miracles. I found myself in a personal experience that contradicted what I believed. I'm in physical, professional, financial, and family crises. I'm trying to figure this out.

What I've learned in my journey of healing is I found myself in a fiery trial where God was releasing grace in my life, but I was also fighting the devil, who was trying to sideline me and take me out. I found myself walking through a story like Job.[1]

Mystery of God's Healing

I have great respect for Bob Sorge's character, his faithfulness, his endurance. He continues to pray and receive prayer for supernatural healing. At this point he still speaks with a whisper, but his voice is heard around the world through his public speaking and books.

I'm choosing to conclude *Healing Rain* with a mystery. Here are questions people have been asking since the time of Job:

- Why do good people suffer?
- Does God make bad things happen?
- Does God heal today?
- If God does heal, why are some healed and others not healed?
- Are miracles real?

The enemy has used examples of times when people haven't received healing or a miracle

- to blame the person for not having enough faith, and
- to make a case that God doesn't heal today.

However, I believe healing is a mystery that we will not understand until heaven. We know that in heaven, believers will be healed of every disease. God will wipe away every tear from the pain we've suffered here on earth (see Revelation 21:4). I don't believe that He causes bad things to happen. However, He uses every circumstance that causes suffering in this world to make us more like Him.

We do know that unconfessed sin can be one obstacle to healing. We are encouraged to confess all sin:

> Is anyone among you sick? Let them call the elders of the church to pray over them and anoint them with oil in the name of the Lord. And the prayer offered in faith will make the sick person well; the Lord will raise them up. If they have sinned, they will be forgiven. Therefore confess your sins to each other and pray for each other so that you may be healed. The prayer of a righteous person is powerful and effective.
>
> James 5:14–16 NIV

Sin blocks every form of healing in our lives. As we confess our sins to one another, we are healed internally and externally.

However, there are times when we walk through things the way Job did. God didn't answer all Job's questions, but He spoke to him out of a whirlwind (see Job 38–41). After Job encountered God, he saw God's majesty, and in the end everything was restored. For those areas in your life where you are still contending for breakthrough, I encourage you to keep going, and don't give up. Encounter God in the midst of your healing journey. He won't fail you.

When I was diagnosed with Hashimoto's thyroiditis, I was told I would likely have to take thyroid medicine all my life. I was told there was no cure. However, as I remained faithful and persevering, God surprised me and healed my thyroid supernaturally. It was just like Him to heal me in a redemptive manner. I originally became sick in Brazil, and it was in Brazil that He chose to heal me of this chronic disease.

Wherever you are on your healing journey, keep believing in the supernatural power of God to be present in your life.

As a healing rain community, let's choose to "rejoice with those who rejoice, and weep with those who weep" (Romans 12:15 NKJV). Let's believe God for signs, wonders, and miracles. Let's also create a safe place for people who are experiencing pain.

Anointing Comes through Pressure

As we conclude, let's focus on immersing ourselves in Christ's love. The word *Christ* comes from the Greek word *chrīstós*, meaning "anointed one." In the Greek Septuagint, the word *Christ* was used to translate the Hebrew, which means "Messiah."

The anointing to heal comes through pressure. What do I mean by that? Think about this: The oil for anointing was made from olives. After olives are harvested, they are washed and pressed. After the pressing, the olive paste is kneaded, and finally, through additional pressure, the oil is extracted. Jesus faced the pressure of the "olive press" at the Garden of Gethsemane, when He overcame the temptation of the enemy through prayer. In a similar way, the hand of God uses the pressure in our lives to purify us and anoint us. His glory and anointing are revealed through this process:

> But we have this treasure in jars of clay to show that this all-surpassing power is from God and not from us. We are hard pressed on every side, but not crushed; perplexed, but not in despair; persecuted, but not abandoned; struck down, but not destroyed. We always carry around in our body the death of Jesus, so that the life of Jesus may also be revealed in our body. For we who are alive are always being given over to death for Jesus' sake, so that his life may also be revealed in our mortal body. So then, death is at work in us, but life is at work in you.
>
> 2 Corinthians 4:7–12 NIV

In these last days, He wants to fill you with "all-surpassing power." He wants to transform you through the process of pressure to make you more like Him.

To be anointed is to be smeared or rubbed with oil. When a person was anointed in the Old Testament, he was anointed as a king, a prophet, or a priest. In the New Testament, the anointing of the Holy Spirit is poured out on all people:

> No matter how many promises God has made, they are "Yes" in Christ. And so through him the "Amen" is spoken by us to the glory of God. Now it is God who makes both us and you stand firm in Christ. He anointed us, set his seal of ownership on us, and put his Spirit in our hearts as a deposit, guaranteeing what is to come.
>
> 2 Corinthians 1:20–22 NIV

God has so many promises for you! He has already said, "Yes." You just need to come into agreement and say, "Amen." He has anointed you and set His seal of the Holy Spirit on your life. The Holy Spirit is a deposit that guarantees God's promises for your future.

Embracing Your First Love

Whatever age or stage you are in, you can be a conduit of healing for others. When you immerse yourself in Christ's love, it will overflow out of you and touch the lives of everyone you come in contact with. The more people you lay hands on and pray over for physical healing, the more people will be miraculously healed. Be on fire with the love of Jesus, and be full of the Holy Spirit.

Wherever you are on your spiritual journey, prioritize your life, as Jesus did. When the Pharisees tried to trap Jesus by asking which of the Ten Commandments was most important, He replied,

> "Love the Lord your God with all your heart and with all your soul and with all your mind." This is the first and greatest commandment. And the second is like it: "Love your neighbor as yourself." All the Law and the Prophets hang on these two commandments.
>
> Mathew 22:37–40 NIV

Immersing yourself in Christ's love will bring balance and wholeness to your mind, your body, and your heart. As you learn to know Christ, the Anointed One, His anointing presence will not only heal the wounds of your heart, but will overflow into the hearts of everyone around you. As you focus on loving God and loving others, supernatural power from heaven will infuse not only your mind and heart, but your body as well.

Healing rain is being poured out in the last days. As we close this healing journey, let's pray together:

> *Beloved Lord,*
> *Your Name is above every name.*
> *You are the Anointed One.*
> *Immerse me in Your presence.*
> *Fill me afresh with Your power.*
>
> *Jesus,*
> *through the pressures of life*
> *I believe You are anointing me*
> *to bring Your healing to others.*
> *I want to know You more.*
> *I want to fellowship with You,*
> *even in suffering.*
>
> *Pour out Your healing rain*
> *on my generation.*

*Use my life as a testimony
of Your transformational love
and supernatural power.
In Your name I pray,
Amen.*

Afterword

A Call for Spiritual Fathers and Mothers

In the previous chapter, you read about Bob Sorge, known as "the speaker who can't talk." Here's what Bob had to say about spiritual mothers and fathers in our *Healing Rain* podcast interview:

> Spiritual children are birthed *en masse*, disciples are made in small groups, spiritual mothers and fathers are fashioned in solitude. When God wants to make you into a spiritual father or mother, He takes you to the wilderness. Moses was in the desert for forty years before God called him through the burning bush. Joshua and Caleb were in the wilderness for forty years before entering the Promised Land. John the Baptist was taken to the wilderness to prepare for the Lord's coming.
>
> To become a spiritual father or mother is a very lonely journey. God will take you through a wilderness of loneliness because He needs your attention.
>
> No one can make a spiritual father or mother. You can make disciples, but you can't make a spiritual father. Only God can fashion a spiritual mother. People can't mentor you to become

a spiritual mother or father; they can mentor you to become a more mature disciple.

To become a spiritual mother or father is not a lesson to be learned. It is a walk that God takes you on. He's not trying to teach you something; He's trying to make you something. He's trying to infuse something into your DNA. He wants you to think differently, walk differently, and respond differently. He's rewriting and reprograming your spiritual DNA. He wants you to be more like Jesus. It's a very intense journey.

When God makes you into a spiritual mother or a spiritual father, He's taking you on a pathway of *earned authority*. Authority in the Kingdom of God is earned in a sense; you've got to do the time. You've got to trudge through that wilderness. Like a general, you have to earn some stars. Authority comes as you walk through your own healing journey with integrity and faithfulness.

The cross was all about *earned authority*. After the cross, Jesus says, "All authority in heaven and earth has been given to me" [see Matthew 28:18]. Jesus was already perfect before the cross. However, before the cross, He couldn't serve as the captain of our salvation or our High Priest. Jesus had to earn His stripes to serve in that kind of capacity. In some of the more noble capabilities in God's Kingdom, you have to earn your stripes.

We need mothers and fathers in the faith who will do the time. Some might say you are in this wilderness because you don't have enough faith. A key word for someone going through a difficult season is *endurance*. Endurance can transform and change you. Just keep walking. Put one foot in front of the other. If you endure great losses in your journey, God will turn them into great victories.[1]

The Making of Spiritual Moms and Dads

Becoming a spiritual mother or father is not about age. Some step into these roles early in their lives. I realize that you may be reading this book in your twenties or thirties and be looking for spiritual moms and dads. You may be looking for someone to pour into your life. However, if you are reading this book and are in your forties or fifties-plus, you are probably nodding your head as you read this. You may already be a spiritual mom or dad who is pouring into the next generation. Or you could be in the midst of God's pressure, being formed into a mature believer. Let me state this:

- The Church is in a spiritual crisis of immaturity.
- Too many have focused on selfish pursuits, are caught in addictions, or are spiritually asleep.
- The Church needs to wake up and repair its nets for revival.
- *You are desperately needed to be a spiritual mother or father in the Kingdom.*

Could it be that the difficult thing you've been walking through is transforming your character to be more like Jesus? Are you willing to lay down your life for the next generation?

In these last days, God is anointing spiritual moms and dads in private to arise in the house of God and in their homes, to bring healing and belonging to a generation of orphans. He has already said "Yes" in heaven. Will you come into an agreement and say "Amen" to your call as a healer to the next generation?

We came to recognize the anointing and authority of Jesus to be our Savior after He endured the cross in His own life.

- Are you willing to pick up your cross and follow Jesus? Are you willing to pay the price for anointing in secret?
- Are you willing to endure disappointment, pain, and loss and allow them to make you better, not bitter?
- Are you willing to embrace your healing journey, holding on to faith in the supernatural?

- Are you willing to be repositioned to make the most difference in the Kingdom of God?
- Are you willing to pour into the next generation sacrificially?
- Are you willing to open your heart and home to make a difference?
- Are you willing to be a portal to heaven's resources that are being given to the next generation?

You can't give something to the next generation that you don't have. You can't earn authority through striving or works of the flesh. God has designed a process of forming spiritual moms and dads that involves their dying to self (see John 12:23–27). Anointing to heal is poured into the DNA of spiritual moms and dads, who bring heaven to earth.

People can wear a badge or title, but they don't necessarily carry the weight of heaven behind their prayers. The question is not your title or position, but rather, *Are you a friend of God?* He's the one who set you apart. You do not have to announce that you are a spiritual dad or mom; those who want to be spiritual kids will seek you out and find you.

Even though I travel most of the time, we have found it important to serve in our local community at UPPERROOM Dallas. The Lord spoke to me and said, *All around you are spiritual sons and daughters; open your heart and home to them.* We began to have young adults over for a meal and ministry. In the brief amount of time since we began, here are some reports we've received of miracles that have resulted:

- One person who made a recommitment to Christ was reconciled with an estranged spouse.
- A young evangelist has been activated in winning people to Jesus.

- A homeless single parent has found community and support.
- One couple has been sent back home and deployed to ministry.
- A husband and wife have found their fit in the ministry.
- A couple who got pregnant before marriage repented, and we led their wedding ceremony with a supportive community around them.
- Many physical healings have taken place, including a newborn's physical heart being mended.
- Many have been equipped and mentored in how to use spiritual gifts.
- Many have been prophesied over and have found new jobs.
- Many are empowered to walk in greater freedom in Christ.
- Many broken hearts have been mended.

Your home can become a portal for heaven's resources being poured out. Are you willing to pay the price to be a healer to the next generation?

Last Days Healing Agents

If God is fashioning you as a spiritual father or mother to carry Christ's anointing of healing in the last days, here are a few characteristics that will be helpful:

- Keep growing and maturing as a son or daughter of Father God. (You can't be a father or mother without first knowing what it is to be a son or daughter.)
- Be a good listener (as well as a good teacher).

- Be flexible, and value individual needs and perspectives. (Many people fall through the gaps of our systems and processes. Learn to go after the one.)
- Be nonreligious and nonjudgmental.
- Be honest and authentic.
- Be a good learner and be vulnerable when you make mistakes.
- Be a carrier of the Word of God and the fire of God.
- Be willing to activate others in supernatural gifts. (Don't allow spiritual kids to put you on a pedestal—you will fall off.)
- Treat others with love, respect, and honor.
- Be willing to correct in love.
- Be available and sacrificial with your time, as the Holy Spirit also guides you in establishing healthy boundaries. (Healthy boundaries help the next generation heal as well.)

These things sound very simple, but they are profound in helping heal the next generation's hearts.

Principles for Establishing a Healing Home

1. *Embrace hospitality, and be willing to be inconvenienced.* Make your house inviting, but invite your spiritual kids into the process. Have them bring food. Invite them to lead worship, be a greeter, or clean up.
2. *Create a safe place for sons and daughters to grow and mature.* Those who come will fall short, and they will sin. Help them overcome sinful choices and habits. Restore them gently, the way you would like to be restored.

3. *Be a place of protection that offers wise counsel.* Let those who come learn from the mistakes you've made over the years, as well as learn to make good choices for themselves. Give wise counsel led by the Spirit.

4. *Provide wise teaching.* This can happen in multiple ways. You could be reading through a book together. You could be challenging the mentality of the age we live in. Know the Word and share it from your heart.

5. *Live a supernatural life.* Invite spiritual sons and daughters into how you hear words of knowledge, prophesy, and pray for the sick. Let them experience the Holy Spirit in your house. Demonstrate what it means to have a portal to heaven, where your home regularly shares the miraculous.

6. *Release spiritual impartation.* Regularly lay hands on the sick and see them recover. Regularly pray for people in transition. Regularly prophesy and share encouraging words.

7. *Release spiritual inheritance.* Your sons and daughters get to stand on your shoulders. They receive a spiritual inheritance from you and others who pour into their lives.

It's redemptive for sons and daughters to be encouraged to fly independently. Be careful with each heart.

- Don't control.
- Don't manipulate.
- Don't exploit others for their gifts.
- Don't be overly critical.
- Don't be unkind.

By the time your spiritual kids are in their twenties, they already have multiple wounds and traumas from church, friends, family, or biological parents. Try not to speak poorly of their biological parents. Help build bridges to their homes of origin. God chose their families. Help build bridges of healing.

I believe you are key to pouring out God's anointing oil on the next generation. Open your heart and your home, and spiritual sons and daughters will come. The next generation is hungry for who you are and what you carry.

Begin a *Healing Rain* Study Group

Jesus empowered His disciples to walk in the miraculous together. If you're looking for a book to study as a group, consider using *Healing Rain* for your next church group or neighborhood group. Use this book to activate your ministry team for personal growth and altar ministry. A *Healing Rain* study group can become a prophetic healing community that actively evangelizes with signs, wonders, and miracles.

As we humbly travel the pathway of God's healing journey together, the anointing of His presence and power multiplies through agreement. As Jesus told us,

> Again I say to you, that if two believers on earth agree [that is, are of one mind, in harmony] about anything that they ask [within the will of God], it will be done for them by My Father in heaven. For where two or three are gathered in My name [meeting together as My followers], I am there among them.
>
> Matthew 18:19–20 AMP

Jesus in Your Midst

The activation and practice of spiritual gifts happen best in small groups. Jesus will be in your midst. As a *Healing Rain* group, you can talk about any of the "Healing Moments for Your Heart and Health" or "Diving Deeper in God's Word" questions or exercises you have found throughout the chapters of this book. But I have also put together a "Group Discussion Guide" for you that is full of discussion questions and bonus activities specifically designed with your group setting in mind. You will find that week-by-week group guide just ahead.

Faith is spelled R-I-S-K. As you see others in your group model gifts like healing, miracles, and prophetic words, you will learn to hear Jesus, too, and you will learn to operate in the gifts, ministering healing rain to others. Being in a prophetic healing community like your small group provides will supercharge your faith.

Weekly Group Schedule

The schedule of your *Healing Rain* group could be as follows:

- **Week 1**: Read the introduction and chapter 1, and complete the questions and activation together. (These weekly activations will happen along with the videos, and the link to those is just ahead.)
- **Week 2**: Read chapters 2–3, and complete the questions and activation.
- **Week 3**: Read chapters 4–5, and complete the questions and activation.
- **Week 4**: Read chapters 6–7, and complete the questions and activation.
- **Week 5**: Read chapters 8–9, and complete the questions and activation.

- **Week 6**: Read chapters 10–11, and complete the questions and activation.
- **Week 7**: Read chapters 12–13, and complete the questions and activation.
- **Week 8**: *Impartation Night!* In preparation for this night of celebration, read chapter 14 and the Afterword. Invite spiritual fathers and mothers to attend, as well as close friends. Share personal testimonies of what Jesus has done in your lives. Create an opportunity for prayers for healing and impartation. Empower new leaders of future *Healing Rain* groups. Make sure words of encouragement are given for each other, and have plenty of food available as you fellowship.

Video Teachings for Your Group

If you would like to go deeper and learn more about the concepts in this book, you can add video teachings to your group experience. As I mentioned in the introduction, I've made a video series available at https://suedetweiler.podia.com/healing-rain-video-course. These videos are instrumental in activating what you are learning as a group each week. Each of the eight videos not only provides deeper biblical foundations for what you are learning, but also models how to walk in the gifts of the Holy Spirit practically. Each video carries an impartation of grace and empowerment. In the video series, you will find practical examples of how to hear the voice of God, how to understand visions from God, how to prophesy, and how to heal the sick.

Group Discussion Guide

WEEK 1

Read: The introduction and chapter 1
Optional: Watch the video "7 Keys to Divine Health." (You will find the ebook mentioned in this group guide on my website, suedetweiler.com. You will also find the *Healing Rain* video course at https://suedetweiler.podia.com/healing-rain-video-course.)

▶ **Group Discussion Questions**

1. What do you hope to gain from this study of *Healing Rain*?
2. Describe a desperate time in your life when you cried out to Jesus for help and He delivered you from oppression.
3. What is your present prayer request? How can this *Healing Rain* group pray for you? Do you have physical issues in your body that need healing? Have you gone through trauma that needs healing?

Bonus: Download my ebook called 7 *Keys to Divine Health*.

WEEK 2

Read: Chapters 2 and 3
Optional: Watch the video "Battle for your Mind."

▶ Group Discussion Questions

1. What new insights have you gained into how your mind impacts your body?
2. As you've thought about and written down potential doors through which the enemy has gained access to your thoughts, have you had any breakthrough revelations? Has the Lord had you get rid of any obstacles in your life that have triggered these thoughts?
3. Has the Lord shown you areas of unprocessed emotions that you've tried to self-medicate to avoid the pain? How do you tend to self-medicate?
4. How can we pray as a group for you this week?

WEEK 3

Read: Chapters 4 and 5
Optional: Watch the video "*Yahweh Rapha*—Our Healer."

▶ Group Discussion and Communion

1. Describe your experience with Communion. Do you take Communion at home?
2. What is your present prayer request? In what areas of your life do you need God's healing?
3. Take Communion together, using the prayers over the bread and the cup that I provided in chapter 5 to pray out loud together as a group. Consider listening to the free

download of the song "Healing Rain" on my website while taking Communion.

WEEK 4

Read: Chapters 6 and 7
Optional: Watch the video "Healing Your Heart."

▶ Group Discussion Questions

1. As you reflect on your last year, what are some of the major disappointments you have faced? What did the Holy Spirit show you about the condition of your heart?

2. What are the promises that God has spoken to your heart? As you positioned your heart to be healed by Jesus, did you have a fresh revelation of Jesus?

3. What "felt needs" came up as you read this week's chapters? How can this *Healing Rain* group pray for you?

WEEK 5

Read: Chapters 8 and 9
Optional: Watch the video "The Power of Forgiveness."

▶ Group Discussion Questions

1. In the "Healing Moments for Your Heart and Health" section at the end of chapter 9, which one of the five personal reflection exercises impacted you the most? Did you experience a fresh surrender to Jesus, a baptism of God's love, forgiveness from the heart? Are you inspired to share your faith with others?

2. Have you ever experienced deliverance in your life? If so, describe the freedom you found in Jesus through it. If

not, is there an area that you believe you need a break-through in?

3. How can this group pray for you this week? Also, do you have a lost friend or a prodigal in your life whom you would like to the group to pray for?

WEEK 6

Read: Chapters 10 and 11
Optional: Watch the video "Faith for Miracles and Healing."

▶ **Group Discussion Questions**

1. How does worship impact you in your healing journey? Are there songs right now that you are worshiping with daily?

2. Describe your times of prayer. Since you've begun this study on healing, have your times of prayer been growing you in greater intimacy with God? Talk about the Scriptures you are standing on for your healing journey. How can we pray for you as a group?

3. Consider taking Communion again together. Before Communion, take a moment to pray out loud the Communion prayers full of declarations of faith in chapter 5. These prayers have great power when read aloud.

WEEK 7

Read: Chapters 12 and 13
Optional: Watch the video "Immersing Yourself in His Transform-ing Presence."

▶ **Group Discussion Questions**

1. What has your experience been of embracing God as your Father? (For some people, talking to God as Father brings up the negative emotions associated with dealing with a harsh, demanding, or even abusive earthly father. Give opportunity for each person in the group to share about this, if applicable.) Has embracing God as a good Father brought healing in your life?

2. As you have been meditating on the nature of God and your access to Him, what new revelation have you gained?

3. Are there things God has called you to let go of? Are there other areas He has called you to embrace more fully, with bold faith?

4. Prepare for Impartation Night: In preparation for next week's special night of celebration, read chapter 14 and especially the afterword. Invite spiritual fathers and mothers to that group meeting, as well as close friends. That night, come prepared to share personal testimonies of what Jesus has done in your lives. Also plan to create an opportunity for prayers of healing and impartation.

WEEK 8

Read: Chapter 14 and the afterword
Optional: Watch the video "Impartation—Encountering Jesus as Healer."

▶ **Closing Group Celebration**

This is a night of food, fellowship, and testimonies. Make everyone feel welcome. Plan ahead of time who will share testimonies. Invite spiritual dads and moms, as well as close friends, to be part of your group for this final meeting. Pray for impartation and healing. Also empower new leaders of future *Healing Rain* groups. Make sure words of encouragement are given for each other, and have plenty of food available as you fellowship.

Notes

Introduction

1. If you would like to read a fuller version of how God delivered us from the fire, see my book *Women Who Move Mountains: Praying with Confidence, Boldness, and Grace* (Minneapolis: Bethany House, 2017).

2. Specifically, you can find the eight-week *Healing Rain* video series at https://suedetweiler.podia.com/healing-rain-video-course.

Chapter 1 Turning Point

1. You can find more valuable resources about health at https://daniwilliam son.com. See also pages 27–46 of her book *Wild & Well* (New York: Morgan James, 2021).

2. You can take the Adverse Childhood Experience (ACE) quiz on multiple Internet sites. This will give you an ACE score that provides further insight into your health. If you have an ACE score of 4 or more, studies show that you are more likely to develop autoimmune disease, cancer, COPD, headaches, heart disease, liver disease, depression, and suicidal tendencies. Whatever your epigenetics, ACE score and current health struggles, Dani's resources, along with the information I'm presenting in *Healing Rain*, will help you turn the tide toward divine health and healing.

Chapter 2 R.E.S.T.

1. Find out more about Dana Candler and her ministry at https://www.dana candler.com.

2. Jenny Splitter, "9 Ways Stress Can Make You Sick," *Everyday Health*, May 19, 2022, https:/www.everydayhealth.com/emotional-health/stress/illnesses -caused-stress/. See also "What Is Stress-Related Illness?" reviewed by Timothy J. Legg, *Healthline*, August 14, 2018, https://www.healthline.com/health/what -is-stress-related-illness.

3. These signs and symptoms of burnout are taken from a message by Pastor Alejandro Morales on June 20, 2022, at a Supernatural Global Network seminar held at King Jesus International Ministry (*Ministerio Internacional El Rey Jesús*) in Miami, Florida.

Chapter 3 Heal Your Head

1. You can find out more about Heidi Mortenson here: https://heidimorten sonlmft.com.

2. Unless otherwise noted, Greek and Hebrew word definitions throughout have been taken from the *NLT New Spirit-Filled Life Bible*, 2nd ed. (Nashville: Thomas Nelson, 2002, 2013), Jack Hayford, executive editor.

Chapter 4 Covenant

1. You can find out more about Sherry Stahl's message and ministry at https://www.sherrystahl.com.

2. Find out more about Joan Hunter's story of being healed of broken heart syndrome in her book *Love Again, Live Again: Restore Your Heart and Regain Your Health* (New Kensington, PA: Whitaker House, 2018).

3. Joan Hunter has authored 25 books and ministers in signs, wonders, and miracles. She leads the 4 Corners Alliance. You can find out more about Joan and her ministry at https://joanhunter.org.

Chapter 5 Gateway

1. You can access the whole 8-week *Healing Rain* video series that goes with this book, including the "7 Keys to Divine Health" segment, here: https://sue detweiler.podia.com/healing-rain-video-course.

2. To learn more about Jewish holidays, I recommend resources from Rabbi Jason Sobel at www.fusionglobal.org. It's from Rabbi Jason that I learned that every milestone in Jesus' life happened on a Jewish holiday.

Chapter 6 A Troubled Heart

1. I'm very grateful for the leadership and teaching of Sharla Brenneman, a pastoral leader serving UPPERROOM and the founder of Inner Room. Her teaching on the heart has impacted my reflections in this section on how the heart is the center of our need for healing. If your heart needs healing, you

can schedule an online appointment with the healing coaches at https://www
.innerroom.co.

2. "The Trap of a Troubled Heart" section is based in part on Michael
Miller's teaching called "Revival Begins in Your Heart," given on October 18,
2019. My son Dre died a few weeks later, on October 30, 2019. Michael and
Lorisa Miller are lead pastors and founders of a prayer and worship movement
called UPPERROOM. You can find the teaching at https://www.youtube.com
/watch?v=slmERgGMgU4.

Chapter 7 Surrender

1. Find out more about the Millers and UPPERROOM Global at https://
www.upperroom.co. Michael has shared this story in several different sermons
over the years. I talked with him about using this story and dream in *Healing
Rain*. You can find one of his sermons here: https://www.youtube.com/watch
?v=slmERgGMgU4.

Chapter 8 Loosed

1. Find out more about Eva and Bill Dooley at http://www.billandevadooley
.com.

2. Find out more about Leslie Tracey and her co-founder of Double Portion
Ministries, Barbara Rucci, at https://dpministries.org. Find out more about
Joan Hunter and 4 Corners Alliance at https://joanhunter.org.

3. One example of contending for healing I saw personally was when I observed Bob Sorge recently at UPPERROOM after he had preached a powerful
message. Bob speaks with a whisper because of a prior injury to his voice. His
heart is so pure, and he walks in incredible spiritual maturity. At the service's
end, he received healing prayers, believing God that he would be physically
healed. You will hear more of his story in chapter 14, and also hear from Bob
in the afterword. I have been impacted by his preaching and teaching, as well
as by his books. Find out more at http://bobsorge.com.

4. To learn more about steps you can take to receive inner healing and
deliverance, you can download a gift called 5 *Steps of Grace: A Journey Guide to
Freedom* on my website, https://suedetweiler.com. Click on the Free Resources
tab.

5. John Wimber led the Vineyard Movement and spoke at healing conferences worldwide. My husband and I were not Vineyard pastors, but we took
all our elders from one of the churches we planted to be trained in healing
at several of his conferences. John is known for his five-step prayer model
for healing. This model dramatically influenced my approach to healing
ministry.

Chapter 9 Freed

1. Find out more about Sean Smith Sr. and R.O.A.R. at https://www.rise ofaremnant.org.

2. Again, you can find this resource at https://suedetweiler.com/free-resou rces/.

Chapter 11 Stand

1. You can find the song "You Make Me Brave" with Amanda Cook here: https://www.youtube.com/watch?v=6Hi-VMxT6fc.

2. You can find the song "Jesus, the Healer" with Lindy Cofer, Elyssa Smith, and the Circuit Riders here: https://youtu.be/2Nkoka4IIeY.

Chapter 12 Wholeness

1. Find out more about Kimberly Stokes at https://www.connectcoach.co.

2. Find out more about Leif Hetland and his ministry at https://global missionawareness.com.

Chapter 14 Anointing to Heal

1. Find out more about Bob Sorge and his books and ministry at http://bob sorge.com. I also encourage you to listen to our whole interview at https://sue detweiler.com/healing-rain-book/.

Afterword

1. Again, find out more about Bob Sorge at http://bobsorge.com.

Sue Detweiler hosts *Healing Rain*, one of the fastest-growing broadcasts on Charisma Podcast Network, listened to in 135 nations. Sue holds a master of divinity degree from Vanderbilt University and is a doctoral student at Global Awakening Theological Seminary. She is part of Randy Clark's Global Awakening Network, and also part of the Supernatural Global Network led by Apostle Guillermo Maldonado. Sue also received the highest recognition from the president of the Foursquare Church, Jack Hayford, for leading Life School of Ministry, a three-year Bible training institute in Nashville that grew to five hundred students.

Sue is a pioneer woman pastor who began preaching at the age of 19. With her husband, Wayne, she planted and co-pastored their first church at the age of 22. With a strong prophetic teaching gift, Sue has equipped men and women to become pastors, evangelists, and missionaries to the nations. She is an international speaker and travels to Central America, South America, Europe, Africa, and the Middle East.

Sue's insights are featured in *Charisma* magazine and on Christian Television Network, Cornerstone Television Network, Son Broadcasting, and regularly on KCBI in Dallas, Texas.

Sue presently serves as the executive director of Life Bridge Global, bringing healing, hope, and freedom to neighbors, nations, and generations. This Christian nonprofit equips individuals, local churches, and international communities through events, training, and creating online media resources, broadcasts, and courses.

Sue and Wayne Detweiler have been married for over thirty-five years and raised six children together. They now have eight grandchildren (and counting).

Subscribe to Sue's podcast *Healing Rain* and to her newsletter.

Other Books and Resources

Other books by Sue are *Women Who Move Mountains: Praying with Confidence, Boldness, and Grace* (Bethany House, 2017), *9 Traits of a Life-Giving Mom* (Morgan James, 2014), and *9 Traits of a Life-Giving Marriage* (Life Bridge Press, 2015). For more information on Sue's books and resources, or to schedule a speaking engagement, visit suedetweiler.com.

Connect with Sue

Instagram: Instagram.com/SueDetweiler
Facebook: Facebook.com/SueDetweiler7
LinkedIn: Linkedin.com/in/suedetweiler
Twitter: Twitter.com/SueDetweiler
Spotify: Healing Rain with Sue Detweiler
Apple Podcasts: Healing Rain with Sue Detweiler
Website: suedetweiler.com

MORE FROM
SUE DETWEILER

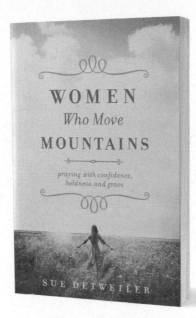

The secret to living and loving well is simple: prayer! So much more than a list of requests, the purpose of prayer is to draw close to God. And when you exchange the obstacles of life for the promises of God, you will pray with passion and confidence. Discover what it means to become a powerful woman of prayer—a source of joy and life to those around you.

Women Who Move Mountains